A Teacher's Guide to

JO DAVID AND DANIEL B. SYME'S

THE BOOK OF THE JEWISH LIFE

Ellen Nemhauser

UAHC Press
New York

CONTENTS

The Book of the Jewish Life and Its Teacher's Guide

ABOUT THE TEXTBOOK AND ITS ORGANIZATION

The Book of the Jewish Life is a textbook about the Jewish life cycle for students in the intermediate grades. Many students will come to this course with some prior knowledge of life-cycle ceremonies from earlier grades in the religious school, as well as from their own experiences at the celebrations of family and friends. This textbook strives to reinforce and enhance basic knowledge about the Jewish life cycle by leading students through a journey of discovery. The richness of the Jewish life cycle, its rituals, blessings, and customs, as experienced through its ceremonies and celebrations, is explored in depth. In addition, the text aims to give students an overview of both the historical background of Jewish life-cycle events and the modern interpretations of these ceremonies and celebrations.

The Book of the Jewish Life consists of nine chapters, which should be taught sequentially from chapters 1 through 9. To cover the material, each textbook chapter requires two to four class sessions.

All the chapters of the textbook are introduced with a **Story**. Each chapter contains at least one **Focus** section to deepen the students' knowledge of the origins, rituals, and customs of each life stage. A section called **Life-Cycle Blessings** presents one or more of the blessings associated with the topic covered by the chapter. The **Text Study** section introduces the origins of the particular life cycle or offers a text that exemplifies the values and ideas embodied in the celebration. Each chapter ends with a Summary of the information presented. The photographs and art enrich the written material and provide opportunities for visual learning.

ABOUT THE TEACHER'S GUIDE

A Teacher's Guide to the Book of the Jewish Life assists teachers in creating a classroom environment where the students can learn and expand their knowledge from the information presented in the textbook. The guide contains activities that closely correspond to the sections within each chapter of the textbook. The teacher's guide supplements the material presented in the textbook, introducing additional legends, laws, customs, and liturgy associated with the Jewish life cycle. The teacher's guide also includes suggestions for students to explore their own family customs and traditions, sharing stories and examining mementos of special times and occasions. This guide includes opportunities for students to explore their own feelings and attitudes about Jewish life-cycle laws and customs by providing exercises for reflection and analysis. Furthermore, students may consider additional and diversified ways in which they can continue to celebrate and mark future Jewish milestones. While the guide does not provide specific lesson plans, it presents a comprehensive selection of activities for the individual teacher to tailor to the particular classroom. This flexible approach allows the teacher to consider such variables as preferred teaching style, student needs, time allocation, and class size. Teachers are encouraged to further supplement this guide with their own ideas and creativity.

Note to the Teacher: When teaching the subject of life cycles, it is particularly important to remember that students come from diverse backgrounds. It is clearly the teacher's job to explore the range of Jewish life-cycle possibilities. At the same time, care must be taken not to bring a student's Jewish identity into question by invalidating the way his or her family celebrates life-cycle events. Remember that the rabbi, cantor, and educator are good resource people to consult in the case of a potentially problematic situation.

HOW THE TEACHER'S GUIDE IS ORGANIZED

Each chapter of the teacher's guide contains the following components:

CHAPTER SUMMARY

A description of the key points presented in the chapter.

INSTRUCTIONAL OBJECTIVES

Objectives for the students to achieve by reading the chapter and engaging in the suggested activities.

KEY TERMS

Definitions of key words and concepts used in

the textbook chapter or as background for study of the chapter. Teachers may choose to distribute a page of terms from this list as a vocabulary or reference sheet. Alternatively, teachers may list the key terms on the blackboard, prior to the class session or as each term is mentioned in the readings or discussion.

OPENING

Suggested introductory activity that will enable the teacher to draw on knowledge that the students already possess, while also introducing them to the new subject matter.

CLASSROOM ACTIVITIES

- Each activity begins with a list of **Materials**, if applicable. This list of supplies will help teachers plan their lessons prior to class by assembling the materials necessary for the selected activities.

- The activities in this section follow the structure of the textbook and should help the teacher guide the students through the text. Not all the activities can or should be undertaken during a single class session. **Teachers must craft a lesson that will be appropriate for their classes based upon their own learning objectives.** At the end of this introduction, there is a general guide to planning a lesson, as well as examples of how a single chapter (in this case, chapter 3) can be structured in two different ways. Critical to successful lesson planning is selecting and balancing a variety of modes of learning such as group work, individual work, written assignments, drama/art/music activities, and discussion. Try to choose activities that complement one another. Aim to craft a lesson that offers sensible and meaningful progression from one activity to the next.

- The first activity of each chapter concentrates on the opening story and is called **Under-**

standing Our Story. The subsequent activities present a variety of ways teachers can engage students in following the textbook.

CHAPTER REVIEW

Final activity, through which teachers can evaluate the students' progress and determine if more time is required to help students learn about a particular life-cycle stage.

CLOSURE

Opportunity for teachers to end one chapter and lead into the next, using a consistent methodology.

JOURNAL ASSIGNMENTS

Opportunity for students to keep a record of their ideas, thoughts, and original prose, as well as stories related to them by relatives, accounts of family traditions, photographs, and their personal commentary. Journal entries are to go in the family albums.

FAMILY ENRICHMENT

Activities sent home by the teacher to enable families to learn together, reinforcing what is being taught in the classroom. Students should keep a small three-ring binder or a pocket-folder for their family albums (how to create a family album is described in chapter 1, p. 15). Students may also add a three-ring plastic envelope (available at any office or paper supply store) in which to collect and protect memorabilia and photos. Later in the school term, teachers may choose to distribute the journal assignments outlined on 8 1/2" x 11" three-hole paper for students to complete and add to their expanding family albums. Teachers should allot time to review Family Enrichment activities in the classroom. All completed Family Enrichment activities should be placed in the album.

IN-CLASS READING STRATEGIES

Many of the activities suggest that teachers have the students read sections of the textbook. There are various ways in which a teacher can accomplish this.

- Ask the students to read aloud, taking turns with each paragraph.
- Pair the students and have them read to each other.
- Have the students read individually; guide their reading by asking questions, including the questions asked in several of the learning activities.
- Assign reading as homework for the students.
- Assign reading as homework for the students and their parents.

RESOURCES

Helpful for teaching a specific life-cycle stage. The following is a list of some publications to help teachers gain a comprehensive understanding of the Jewish life cycle in general, its laws, customs, traditions, and contemporary practices:

Abromowitz, Yossi, and Susan Silverman. *Jewish Family and Life*. New York: Golden Books, 1997.

Diamant, Anita, and Howard Cooper. *Living a Jewish Life: A Guide for Starting, Learning, Celebrating, & Parenting*. New York: HarperCollins Publishers, 1991.

Donin, Hayim. *To Be a Jew: A Guide to Jewish Observance in Contemporary Life*. New York: Basic Books, 1991.

Dosick, Rabbi Wayne. Living Judaism: *The Complete Guide to Jewish Belief, Tradition, and Practice*. San Francisco: Harper, 1995.

Kolatch, Alfred J. *The Jewish Book of Why, Volumes I, II, & III*. Middle Village, New York: Jonathan David Publishers Inc., 1981.

Lieberman, Susan. *New Traditions: Redefining*

Celebrations for Today's Family. New York: Farrar, Straus & Giroux, 1991.

Maslin, Simeon, ed. *Gates of Mitzvah (Shaarei Mitzvah): A Guide to the Jewish Life Cycle*. New York: CCAR Press, 1979.

Olitzky, Kerry M., and Ronald H. Isaacs. *The How-to Handbook for Jewish Living*. Hoboken, N.J.: Ktav Publishing House, Inc., 1993.

Orenstein, Debra, ed. *Lifecycles, Volume One: Jewish Women on Life Passages and Personal Milestones*. Woodstock, VT.: Jewish Lights Publishing, 1994.

_____*Lifecycles, Volume Two: Jewish Women on Life Themes and Cycles of Meaning*. Woodstock, VT.: Jewish Lights Publishing, 1996.

Roth, Cecil and Geoffrey Wigoder. *Encyclopaedia Judaica*. Philadelphia: Keter Publishing, 1994.

Samuel, Edith. *Your Jewish Lexicon*. New York: UAHC Press, 1982.

Stern, Chaim, ed. *On the Doorposts of Your House (Al Mezuzot Beitecha): Prayers and Ceremonies for the Jewish Home*. New York: CCAR Press, 1994.

Syme, Daniel B. *The Jewish Home: A Guide for Jewish Living*. New York: UAHC Press, 1988.

SETTING THE STAGE

Creating a stimulating learning environment sets the stage for the lesson. Decorate the classroom with photographs, photocopies, and drawings of Jewish life-cycle events and related ritual objects. These can be obtained from the *Encyclopaedia Judaica*, Jewish calendars, Jewish books and catalogues, and on the Internet.

LESSON PLANNING

Below are examples of how the same chapter in the textbook can be presented in two different ways, based upon different instructional objectives and using a different selection of activities from among those given in the teacher's guide. Teachers are encouraged to develop their own instructional objectives and to select those activities that best support the desired outcomes. Appendix sheet 1 (p. 77) is a sample lesson planner form that may be reproduced and is designed to help the teacher develop an organized, coherent lesson plan for each chapter of *The Book of the Jewish Life*.

Sample Lesson Plan 1
for Chapter Three

Joining the Jewish Community

(Note: This lesson requires 75 minutes of class time.)

Focus

In this lesson, the students will explore traditional and contemporary ways in which new babies and converts are welcomed into the covenant of the Jewish people.

Instructional Objectives

Students will be able to:

1. List ways in which they can act as "guarantors" for the Jewish people.
2. List three ceremonies for welcoming new members into the covenant of the Jewish people.
3. Compare and contrast the liturgy used at the birth of a baby.
4. Discuss the events that take place at the *Berit Bat* and *Berit Milah* ceremonies.

Materials: Copies of *On the Doorposts of Your House* (New York: CCAR Press, 1994), pp. 109-110.

LESSON

Opening (5 minutes)
(See Opening on p. 26 of chapter 3.)

Classroom Activities
Understanding Our Story (10 minutes)
Blessing for the Moment of Birth (15 minutes)
Berit Ceremonies (20 minutes)

Chapter Review (5 minutes)
(See Chapter Review on p. 30 of chapter 3.)

Closure (5 minutes)
(See Closure on p. 30 of chapter 3.)

Family Enrichment Activity Berit Ceremonies in My Family.

Sample Lesson Plan 2
for Chapter Three

Joining the Jewish Community

(Note: This lesson requires 75 minutes of class time.)

Focus

In this lesson, the students will explore traditional and contempory ways in which new babies and converts are welcomed into the covenant of the Jewish people.

Instructional Objectives:

Students will be able to:

1. List three ceremonies for welcoming new members into the covenant of the Jewish people.
2. Discuss the events that take place at the *Berit Bat* and *Berit Milah* ceremonies.
3. Recognize the Torah text that describes the first *Berit Milah*.
4. Identify the ways in which people prepare for conversion to Judaism.

Materials: Guest(s) to speak about conversion to Judaism; list of questions for guests prepared by students.

LESSON

Opening (5 minutes)
(see opening on p. 26 of chapter 3.)

Classroom Activities
Berit Ceremonies—The History of Circumcision (10 minutes)

Conversion—Another Way of Joining the Jewish Community (30 minutes)

Chapter Review (5 minutes)
(See Review on p. 30 of chapter 3.)

Closure (5 minutes)
(See Closure on p. 30 of chapter 3.)

Family Enrichment: You Are the Teacher.

Cycles from Generation to Generation

CHAPTER SUMMARY

The first chapter of *The Book of the Jewish Life* explores the concept of cycles and how Judaism provides us with rituals to celebrate the key moments in our life cycle.

INSTRUCTIONAL OBJECTIVES

1. Survey the Jewish life cycle by examining some of the rituals that mark the stages of a Jewish individual's life.

2. Explore the concept of *le'dor vador*, literally, "generation to generation," and discover the ways in which life-cycle rituals help connect one generation of the Jewish people to both past and future generations.

3. Understand that the links between generations help ensure Jewish continuity.

4. Examine various Jewish texts that highlight the concept of life cycle, including the Ve'ahavta prayer.

KEY TERMS

Le'dor vador	"from generation to generation"; the Jewish concept of passing on our heritage from one generation to the next.
Family tree	A diagram of family relationships, usually spanning several generations.
Genealogy	The study of the generations of one's family.
Generation	A group of individuals constituting a single stage in a line of descent.
Life cycle	The cycle of life from birth to death, during which transitions are marked by specific celebrations and rituals.
Namesake	The person for whom one is named.
Ritual	A formal act or series of acts involving religious symbols, prayers, and blessings.

OPENING

ALL LIVING THINGS HAVE A CYCLE
(15 minutes)

Materials: Life-cycle diagram; tape or CD player; tape recording of "Turn, Turn, Turn" or "The Circle Game"; handouts with song lyrics.

1. Draw a large circle on posterboard or mural paper. In the center write "The Jewish Life Cycle." Divide the circle into ten sections (one space for each chapter, plus one extra).

2. Ask the students to define "life cycle." Record their answers in one of the sections on "The Jewish Life Cycle" diagram. Ask them what in our world has cycles. [solar system, seasons, washing machines, human beings, agriculture, etc.]

3. Tell the students that in this unit they will explore Jewish rituals that mark the stages in a person's life. They will learn that Jewish tradition teaches that life is a cycle from beginning to end and from generation to generation. Each stage is sacred and needs to be consecrated in a special way.

4. Ask the students to suggest ways in which the life cycle of a Jewish person may differ from that of a person of another faith. Students may suggest some of the actual life-cycle ceremonies that Jews celebrate, or they may say that Jews mark life-cycle stages in their synagogue communities, using specifically Jewish texts and customs.

5. Conclude by playing a tape of the song "Turn, Turn, Turn" or "The Circle Game."

6. Distribute the lyrics and ask the students to reflect on the way the song represents the concept of a life cycle.

CLASSROOM ACTIVITIES

UNDERSTANDING OUR STORY
(20 minutes)

Materials: Sheets of ruled paper.

1. Have the students read the "A Tree for David" story on p. 2 of the textbook.

2. Ask the students how the old man in the story thought ahead to future generations. [It was his family's tradition for each person to plant a tree for a future namesake.]

3. Explain that planting a tree is only one way for a person or family to provide for future generations.

4. Have the students work independently to create a special way to think ahead for future generations. At the top of a blank sheet of paper have each student write: "Actions I Can Take to Help Future Jewish Generations." Give the students several moments to generate three or four ideas each.

5. Have the students share their ideas with the class. If the ideas are practical and realistic, the class can vote to adopt one or two of the students' ideas as a class project.

Note: This activity can also be done as a time capsule project with the students being asked to place pictures and/or objects in a sealed container to be opened in 100 years. Invite them to choose things they feel are vital to Jewish survival. Ask the students to share their selections, and write their choices on the board.

TEXT STUDY
(20 minutes)

Materials: Copies of Ecclesiastes 3:1-8.

1. Have the students read through Ecclesiastes 3:1-8 on page 4 of the textbook.

2. Invite different students to read successive verses.

3. Lead the class in a discussion of what the biblical author might have meant with these words. [E.g.: The author was speaking about the balances in life, the contrasts in our world, and the fact that one must confront a whole range of experiences to live a full life.]

4. Ask the students to suggest new themes by adding additional verses that are meaningful to them. Allow time for the students to write their additional verses in their journals.

5. If there is time, the class can share their ideas for additional verses.

FOCUS: LIFE CYCLES— A SPECIAL TYPE OF CYCLE
(30 minutes)

Materials: Copies of Genesis 1:2-4; writing paper; pencils; construction paper; glue.

1. Have the students read the Focus section "Life Cycles—A Special Type of Cycle" on page 5 of the textbook.
2. Remind the students that there are many kinds of cycles in our world.
3. Tell the students that according to tradition, it was God who set our world and each of its cycles in motion.
4. Instruct the students to read the opening of Parashat Bereshit, Genesis 1:1-2:4.
5. Ask the students to draw a two-column chart. On one side, have them list the steps of creation as described in the parashah. On the opposite side, have the students list the cycles that were set in motion by each of God's creations. Tell the students that some days may have more than one cycle and some days none at all. Give the students at least one example as a trigger. (See the examples below.)

Creation	Cycles
Light	Planetary and Solar/Lunar
Sky	Weather; Seasons
Earth and Sea, Plants and Trees	Time; Life and Death; Tides; Seasons; Agriculture
Sun, Moon, Stars to separate Day and Night	Calendar; Solar/Lunar
Birds, Creeping Creatures, Fish	Reproduction; Evolution
Beasts of the Earth	Evolution
Humanity	Ignorance then Knowledge, War and Peace
Shabbat	Work and Rest

6. Create a master list on the board.
7. Discuss the list and point out how each element of God's creation has a corresponding system or cycle to make it ordered and regular.
8. Have the students identify the cycles that are completely beyond human control and those over which we do exercise some power. Ask the students what this tension implies [E.g.: There is a partnership between God and humankind in which we work together to make sense of the world by giving order to life.]
9. Stress the fact that Jewish life-cycle ceremonies emphasize the relationship between God and human beings and that the rituals associated with each stage seek to deepen the meaning of our lives and reaffirm our connection to and involvement in God's creative process. This point can be illustrated further by asking the students to imagine a world without distinct cycles.
10. Discuss how it would feel to live without order and systems, in what the Torah (Genesis 1:2) calls **tohu vavohu**, literally, "unformed and void."
11. Divide another piece of paper in half. On one half, have the students use torn paper and glue to make a collage of the world before order existed; on the other half, have them make a collage of the world after order is created.

THE JEWISH LIFE CYCLE AND ITS RITUALS
(10 minutes)

Materials: Writing paper and pencils.

1. Have the students turn to page 6 of the textbook.
2. Explain that the italic headings in blue are the life cycles that will be studied throughout this unit and the bulleted items are the rituals associated with those life cycles.

3. Allow time for the students to review the contents of the page.

4. Ask the students if they have any initial questions or concerns about what they will be studying.

5. The students may write their questions or concerns on pieces of paper.

6. Collect the slips, divide the comments into their corresponding chapters, and address the issues as the class studies that particular section. These slips of paper will provide you with information about what is important and of concern to the students, thus aiding in directing future lessons.

INTRODUCING GENERATIONS

1. Have the students explain the Hebrew term *dor*, or, in English, "generation."

2. Have the students read the section "Repeating Life-Cycle Rituals—Introducing Generations" on page 7 of the textbook.

3. Explain to the students that while the text teaches that one generation is twenty years, most of our parents married and had children when they were older. Therefore, the span from one generation to the next is actually longer than twenty years.

4. Ask the students if they have heard the term *generation gap*. Invite them to suggest examples of uses of the phrase.

5. Ask the students in what ways there might be a *Jewish* generation gap. Is there a gap between themselves and their parents or between themselves and their grandparents? Why might one generation have a hard time understanding and relating to the Judaism of a different generation? Ask the students to give specific examples of Jewish generation gaps.

FAMILY TREES
(20 minutes and time at home to do research)

Materials: Large pieces of blank white paper for each student, rulers, pencils, materials for decoration.

1. Have students work in small groups to study the family tree of Abraham and Sarah on page 9 of the textbook.

2. Point out the biblical verses that provide the evidence for this family tree: Genesis 11:27-32; 16:15-16; 21:1-3; 24:67; 25:1-4; 25:12-15; 25:19-26. (Teachers may omit those verses they consider less essential to the narrative plot.)

3. Instruct the students to draft a template they can use to complete the construction of their own family trees. Remind them that just as Abraham and Sarah's family tree was unique, their own template will need to be "tailor made" for their own particular family arrangement (e.g., stepparent, half-siblings). Point out that they may discover someone they did not know existed as they interview family members for this assignment.

4. Have the students complete their family trees at home. Remind them to bring the trees back to school for the next class.

5. Encourage the students to collect as much information as possible about each member on the tree (e.g., the Hebrew name, place of birth, occupation).

6. Later the trees can be decorated and displayed in the classroom.

LEDOR VADOR
(10 minutes)

Materials: Writing paper and pencils.

1. Have the students choose a photograph from either page 7 or page 8 of the textbook.

2. Ask them to examine either photograph and write a short diary entry from the perspective of one of the family members shown in the picture.

3. The paragraph should express some of the thoughts and emotions that the student imagines the person in the picture is thinking or feeling.

4. Tell the students to include the expression *ledor vador* in their paragraph.

FAMILY ALBUM
(20 minutes)

Materials: Binders or Pocket-folders; twenty sheets of ruled paper; ten sheets of construction paper for each student; a three-hole punch; materials to decorate the covers of the pocket-folders.

1. Provide each student with a three-ring binder or folder, ten sheets of three-ringed 8 1/2" x 11" construction paper, and twenty sheets of three-ringed ruled paper.
2. Instruct the students to alternate pieces of ruled paper and construction paper and insert them into their binder. The students will create family albums, in which they will write short journal entries and paste photos and memorabilia.
3. Provide the students with materials to decorate the cover of their new family album.

INTERGENERATIONAL ACTIVITY
(45 minutes)

1. Invite some senior members of the community to class. There may be a seniors' club in the synagogue or in the larger Jewish community or arrange with parents for some of the students' grandparents to come to class.
2. Ask the visitors to prepare for the visit by reading the opening chapters of the textbook.
3. Request that the visitors bring meaningful Jewish artifacts and memorabilia from their own lives. These should be items about which a story can be told (preferably one with Jewish themes and details).
4. Allow the visitors a specified amount of time in which to present their meaningful item and story.
5. Allow for a question-and-answer period when they have finished their presentations.

CLOSURE

Materials: Life-cycle diagram.

1. Review with the students the concepts and terms that were explored in this chapter (e.g., Jewish cycle, life cycle, and ledor vador). Write the terms in one of the sections of the "Life Cycle" diagram. (As the class works its way through the topics, you will fill in the appropriate space with phrases, words, and pictures that represent their understanding of the particular time on the life cycle.)
2. Ask the students if anything surprised them in their reading. Ask them if anything was already familiar.
3. Continue by asking the students to raise their hands if they can write their names in Hebrew.
4. Have the students find out their Hebrew names and learn how to write them for the next session, which will explore the rituals surrounding Jewish naming.

FAMILY ENRICHMENT

JOURNAL WRITING

1. Send the students home with a copy of the journal assignment from appendix sheet 2 (p. 79).
2. The students will investigate some of their family traditions. By learning more about the past generations of their families and how those relatives celebrated the special stages of their lives, the students will understand more clearly how and why certain family customs developed, getting ideas to help develop new and meaningful life-cycle rituals of their own.
3. Instruct the students to interview their parents, grandparents, aunts, uncles, cousins and close family friends using the journal assignment worksheet.
4. Remind the students that even if some relatives are no longer alive, others will be able to help them with stories and facts.
5. When they have completed the worksheet, they will have discovered much about their

families and how important traditions and customs have been passed along to subsequent generations.

6. Have the students record any other questions of interest.

7. Invite them to reflect on ways in which they can ensure that future generations can learn about the present time and their family in this generation.

TREE PLANTING

1. Have the students and their families plant a tree (indoors or outdoors depending on their demographics and housing situation) in honor of future generations.

2. Suggest readings and texts from Molly Cone's *Listen to the Trees*, (New York: UAHC Press, 1996). Encourage families to take photographs of their trees, the planting, and their ceremonies.

3. Ask the students to report on their ceremonies in class and show their photographs.

4. Create a display of the photographs with captions written by the students.

RESOURCES

Rottenberg, Dan. *Finding our Fathers—A Guide to Jewish Genealogy*. New York: Random House, 1977.

Wolfman, Ira. *Do People Grow on Family Trees?* New York: Workman Publishing Co., 1991.

http://www.Jewishgen.org/—for help in Jewish genealogy.

Birth and Naming

CHAPTER SUMMARY

This chapter explores the past and present customs of Jewish naming. Students will discuss the significance of their Hebrew names, study formal naming ceremonies, and examine what to do when one does not receive a Hebrew name at birth.

INSTRUCTIONAL OBJECTIVES

1. Enable the students to know their Hebrew names in written form.
2. Discuss the significance of the students' Hebrew names.
3. Examine the names of various biblical figures and discuss several examples of characters who underwent name changes.
4. Explore several ways that Hebrew names are chosen for babies and Jews-by-choice.

KEY TERMS

Ashkenazic Jews Jews from Eastern and Northern Europe.

Birkat Hagomel Literally, "Blessing of the Rescued"; the special blessing recited during the Torah service by a person who has survived a dangerous situation.

Diaspora Living outside the State of Israel.

Hiddur mitzvah A rabbinic principle that teaches the value of embellishing and enhancing an object used for performing a ritual *mitzvah*.

Mi Sheberach Literally, "May the One who blesses"; the special blessing recited during the Torah service in which God's name is invoked for blessing on a person at the time of a special occasion or in honor of a significant event.

Sephardic Jews Originally Jews from parts of Southern and Western Europe, like Spain, Portugal, and other countries in the Mediterranean region. Later the term came to be used also for Jews from North Africa.

Shehecheyanu Literally, "the One who has kept us alive"; the blessing said at all "first" occasions and other very special moments in a person's life.

OPENING
(10 minutes)

Materials: Index cards and pencils.

1. Distribute index cards to students as they enter the classroom.
2. Instruct students to write five names or desig-

nations by which they can be identified. (E.g.: My name is Ms. Cohen, but I'm also "teacher," "Marc's sister," "volleyball player," "dog walker," etc.)

3. Allow three to five minutes for students to work alone.

4. Collect and shuffle the cards, mixing the order several times.

5. Using all the designations except the students' names, read aloud the contents of a few cards and allow students to guess "who's who."

6. At the end of the activity, explain to the students that people's identities are complex and that individuals can be recognized in many ways. In Hebrew we are known as "son of X and Y" or "daughter of X and Y." Sometimes names reflect a person's traits, personality, or interests (like with nicknames). Sometimes names are assigned according to profession (like with Jews in Europe) or by accident (like with many Jews who immigrated to the United States).

7. Instruct the students that today the class is going to explore the significance of naming and do some research into the students' own names.

CLASSROOM ACTIVITIES

UNDERSTANDING OUR STORY
(10 minutes)

Materials: Bibles

1. Have the students read the story "It's Easy If You Know the Secret" on pages 12-13 of the textbook.

2. Point out the verses of Torah (Genesis 2:19-20) that may have led to this story.

3. Ask students if they think the story reflects the actual way the ancients named animals and other things they encountered.

4. Ask the students to state the "secret" of naming as suggested by the story. Students

should also be asked to consider God's role in the process of naming things.

5. Discuss experiences the students have had with selecting a name for pets, siblings, stuffed animals, dolls, boats, etc. How did they make their final choice? What other name could they have chosen? Did the name continue to seem appropriate over time?

FOCUS: WHAT'S IN A NAME?
(20 minutes)

Materials: Bibles; a Hebrew/English name dictionary.

1. Ask the students to write their names vertically down the side of a piece of paper.

2. Instruct the students to use the first letter of each line to begin a word or phrase that characterizes their personality or appearance.

3. Have the students read the Focus section "What's in a Name?" on pages 13-14 of the textbook.

4. Discuss the message of the text from the midrash that is mentioned in this section.

5. Ask the students to write their Hebrew names at the top of the back of their pieces of paper. Instruct them to list the numbers 1, 2, 3 down the left side of the page.

6. Tell the students to suggest three names for themselves, corresponding to the message of the text from *Ecclesiastes Rabbah*. The first should "name" the qualities their parents wish for them; the second should "name" the things others see in them; and the third should be a name for what they themselves value most about their own character.

7. Allow the students to share their ideas.

8. Explain to the students that Jewish tradition places great importance on naming.

9. Ask the students to suggest possible reasons for this.

TEXT STUDY

(15 minutes)

Materials: Bibles; a Hebrew/English name dictionary.

1. Have the students go over the items in the Text Study section on pages 14-15 of the textbook.

2. Explain that names in the Bible have special meaning and can often reflect the narrative's plot.

3. Divide the students into small groups to examine various narrative sections chosen from the list below.
   - Rachel naming her handmaiden's sons: Genesis 30:5-8
   - Leah naming her handmaiden's sons: Genesis 30:10-13
   - Leah naming her children: Genesis 30:18-21
   - Naming of Jacob and Esau: Genesis 25:25-26

4. Ask the students to report their findings to the whole class using the blackboard or chart paper to list the biblical names they encounter.

5. Instruct the students to explain the significance of the names in the narrative. (Students may require assistance connecting the Hebrew names to their Hebrew meanings.)

BIBLICAL NAME CHANGES

(15 minutes)

1. In the Bible, names were so representative of a person's affiliation (even today there are those people who believe certain names are indicative of a person's ethnic or religious affiliation) that several who experienced a fundamental change of identity also underwent a name change.

2. Ask the students to examine these passages that deal with name changes:

   Abram = Abraham: Genesis 17:5

   Sarai = Sarah: Genesis 17:15-16

   Jacob = Israel: Genesis 32:23-29

   Hoshea = Joshua: Numbers 13:16
   (for an explanation on this particular name change, consult W. Gunther Plaut, *The Torah, A Modern Commentary* [New York: UAHC Press, 1981].

3. Discuss with the students the events that prompted the name changes in these biblical characters.

4. Ask the students if there are any occasions when people in our modern society change their names. [getting married, converting, gaining a title such as rabbi, RJE, or Dr.]

5. Ask the students to explain in their own words the significance of changing one's name.

FOCUS: CHOOSING A HEBREW NAME

(15 minutes)

Materials: Writing paper and pencils.

1. Have the students read the Focus section "Choosing a Hebrew Name" on page 16 of the textbook.

2. Ask the students if their Hebrew name honors a relative.

3. Have the students share some information about their namesake.

4. Ask the students if their parents are descended from the Ashkenazic or Sephardic tradition.

5. For homework, have the students investigate the person for whom they were named (see Family Enrichment, "Investigating My Hebrew Name," p. 23).

6. Guide the students to develop of a list of questions that can be used to interview their parents, grandparents, and other family members. Have those students who are not

named for a relative investigate the meaning of their name, its origin, characters from Jewish history with the same name, the reasons their parents chose that particular name, and similar questions. Help the students develop an interview of eight to ten questions to reveal a broad range of details about the person for whom they were named. [E.g.: Where did he/she live? What was his/her occupation? For what particular things was she/he known? What was his/her involvement in the Jewish community?] This exercise can be done for both a first and middle name. In addition, where the students have Hebrew and English names from different namesakes, the Hebrew and English names can both be investigated.

Jewish Naming Ceremonies and Certificates
(10 minutes)

Materials: Writing paper and pencils.

1. Have the students read the section "*Jewish Naming Ceremonies and Certificates*" on page 17 of the textbook.

2. Ask the students to write a short paragraph that describes the action taking place in the photograph on page 17 of the textbook.

3. Encourage the students to use their imagination to write about the thoughts and feelings of the parents as they name their daughter at her Berit Bat.

4. Share the various answers.

5. Have the students look at the picture of the child-naming certificate on the bottom of page 17 of the textbook. Discuss the images on the certificate and the meanings they suggest. [Noah's ark, the end of the Flood, the rainbow as the sign of God's covenant] How do these illustrations relate to the thoughts of parents at the time of a child's naming?

Life-Cycle Blessings: Shehecheyanu
(15 minutes)

Materials: Copies of Blessings.

1. Ask the students if they are familiar with the *Shehecheyanu* blessing (*Gates of Prayer*, p. 451) and have a volunteer recite or lead the class in singing the blessing.

2. Ask the class when this blessing is said. [first night of Chanukah, bar/bat mitzvah ceremonies, and all new beginnings]

3. Tell the students that in a naming ceremony, the Shehecheyanu is recited. Have the students read the first paragraph of "Life-Cycle Blessings" on page 18 of the textbook.

4. Consider teaching the text in the form of a song. A few different versions are available in recordings and in sheet music from Transcontinental Music Publishing. (Where possible, the cantor or music teacher can come to class for this segment.)

Life-Cycle Blessings: Mi Sheberach
(10 minutes)

Materials: Copies of blessings.

1. Explain to the students that in some instances people may choose to formally name their new child at the Torah service during worship. In those instances, the rabbi or cantor may recite a traditional blessing called *Mi Sheberach*.

2. Explain that because Hebrew uses masculine and feminine pronouns, adjectives, nouns, and verbs, the blessings are slightly different for girls and boys.

3. Have the students read the second and third paragraphs of Life-Cycle Blessings on page 18 of the textbook.

4. Ask the students to enumerate the differences in the blessings for a boy and for a girl.

LIFE-CYCLE BLESSINGS: *BIRKAT HAGOMEL*
(10 minutes)

Materials: Copies of blessings.

1. Explain to students that there is a tradition for saying a blessing when you have come through a time of danger and you are safe once again. A new mother may choose to recite the *Birkat Hagomel* once she has begun to recover from giving birth. Ask students what they think might be in the contents of this prayer. Remind students that the blessing is not solely for childbirth, rather, it may be said after any dangerous situation has passed.

2. Now look at the actual blessing on page 19 of the textbook.

3. Ask the students if any of the contents of the actual prayer surprises them and if so, why?

HIDDUR MITZVAH
(20 minutes)

Materials: Samples of Jewish naming certificates; markers; crayons; construction paper; glue; tissue paper.

1. After the students read the section "Jewish Naming Ceremonies and Certificates" on page 17 of the textbook, have the students create beautiful naming certificates.

2. Explain the concept of *hiddur mitzvah*, which teaches that it is a *mitzvah* to embellish and enhance an object used in carrying out a ritual *mitzvah*. For example, one is encouraged, whenever possible, to use a special and beautiful cup for the *Kiddush* blessing rather than using a paper cup. In this case the *mitzvah* of naming a child in the Jewish tradition is embellished and enhanced by a beautiful certificate that can be framed, displayed, and cherished forever. Teachers

may obtain samples of naming certificates from the rabbi, Jewish catalog companies, or Jewish gift shops. Some students may be able to bring their own naming certificates for display in the classroom.

3. Distribute supplies to the students.

4. Encourage students to think about what Jewish symbols to use in their creations.

5. The students can fill in the certificates for themselves or another member of their family. A perpetual Jewish calendar will be useful in determining Hebrew birth dates.

VIDEO SESSION
(45 minutes)

Materials: "The Eighth Day" (Video, VCR).

1. Preview the video "The Eighth Day." This is readily available in Jewish media resource libraries, your synagogue, or the school library, or it can be ordered from Ergo Media, 800-695-ERGO.

2. Once you have viewed the video, show it to the class.

3. Ask the class for comments. Why was *Berit Milah* important enough for this family to risk their life to continue the ritual? What choice would the students have made given the same set of circumstances?

PHOTO MATCH-UP GAME
(15 minutes)

Materials: Photographs or color photocopies; Velcro; posterboard; instant camera and film.

1. Ask each student to bring in a photograph or color photocopy of a picture from when they were a baby.

2. Take a current photograph of each child with the instant camera and film.

3. Attach one side of the Velcro to each baby picture and to each current photograph. Attach the other side of the Velcro to the

posterboard, leaving enough space around each one to attach the photographs.

4. Attach the current photographs to the Velcro on the board.

5. Give each student someone else's baby picture, and have them match up the baby picture with the current photo.

OUR FULL HEBREW NAMES
(15 minutes)

Materials: Copies of Hebrew name worksheet (appendix sheet 3); a Hebrew/English name dictionary.

1. Explain to the students that their full Hebrew names have three parts as follows:

    Part 1—the Hebrew first name they were given

    Part 2—one parent's Hebrew first name

    Part 3—their other parent's Hebrew first name

    Example:

    Part 1—A student's Hebrew name is Yitzchak.

    Part 2—His father's name is Mosheh.

    Part 3—His mother's name is Rivkah.

    His complete Hebrew name is: **Yitzchak ben Mosheh veRivkah**.

2. Hand students a copy of the Hebrew name worksheet from appendix sheet 3 (p. 80).

3. Students may need assistance in Hebrew spelling. Teachers should have a Jewish naming book with Hebrew names on hand to check spelling and to help students determine the literal meaning of their Hebrew names.

CHAPTER REVIEW
(5 minutes)

1. Write the term "Naming" on the board.

2. Ask the students to help make a list of ways that Jews choose Hebrew and English names for their children.

3. Invite the students to discuss the significance of their Hebrew names.

4. Ask the students what they know so far about naming ceremonies.

5. Tell the students that in the next lesson they will learn more about other naming ceremonies.

CLOSURE
(15 minutes)

1. Ask students to recall the various ways in which Hebrew names are chosen for a baby, by someone converting to Judaism, or by someone who has never been given a Hebrew name and desires to do so later in life. (Emphasize that there is no one right way.)

2. Add terms and concepts related to this stage of the life cycle to "The Jewish Life-Cycle" diagram.

3. Assign the students a family activity. If students are going to use the interview tool developed by the class in Focus activity #6 on page 19, be sure to have copies to distribute to each student.

JOURNAL ASSIGNMENT

Have students complete one of the following phrases with a short paragraph.

1. Investigating the meaning of my Hebrew name has made me feel _____

   _____.

2. I think it's important to have a name representing some aspect of my character because _____

   _____.

3. Were I to add to or change my name like some of the biblical characters we studied, I would choose for myself the name _____

   _____ because_____

   _____.

FAMILY ENRICHMENT

INVESTIGATING MY HEBREW NAME

1. Instruct the students to investigate the person for whom they were named.

2. Where applicable, they can use the list of questions developed by the class in Focus activity #6 on page 19.

3. Encourage students to interview as many family members as possible, since different people may have a variety of perspectives on the person's character, disposition, features, strengths, achievements, etc.

4. Where possible, students should attach a photograph of themselves and a photograph of the person after whom they are named o their report.

5. The reports should be added to the students' family album.

FAMILY CREST ACTIVITY

1. Students and their families can work together to create a family crest. They may wish to examine other family crests in encyclopedias to get ideas.

2. Their own creation should include a symbol of the family's place of origin, artwork that is symbolic of unique family stories or traits, illustrations of any special family sports or activities, pets, hobbies, etc.

3. Students should add any illustrations created by their family to their family album.

RESOURCES

Diamant, Anita. *The New Jewish Baby Book: Names, Ceremonies, and Customs for Today's Families*. Woodstock, Vt.: Jewish Lights Publishing, 1993.

Plaut, W. Gunther. "Identity and Name." In *The Torah: A Modern Commentary*. UAHC Press, 1981, p. 119.

Joining the Jewish Community

CHAPTER SUMMARY

This chapter explores the ways in which new babies or Jews by choice are welcomed into the Jewish community. The traditional rite of *Berit Milah*, the relatively new custom of *Berit Bat,* and aspects of the conversion ceremony are described.

INSTRUCTIONAL OBJECTIVES

1. Explore three ceremonies for welcoming those becoming new members of the Jewish people: *Berit Milah*, *Berit Bat*, and conversion, in addition to other rituals that celebrate new life.
2. Compare and contrast those ceremonies of welcome.
3. Examine the text of *Berit Milah* and consider the modern ideals that led to the modification of the rite in the Reform movement.

KEY TERMS

Aliyah latorah literally "going up to the Torah;" the honor of reciting the blessings before or after the reading of Torah during the worship service.

Berit Literally, "covenant;" a pact or agreement between two or more individuals or parties.

Berit Bat The ritual of welcoming a baby girl into the covenant of the Jewish people.

Berit Milah Literally, the covenant of circumcision; the ritual mitzvah of circumcising the foreskin of the penis that a newborn boy undergoes. *Berit Milah* is traditionally also part of conversion to Judaism for any male.

Birkat Hamazon A series of blessings said at the conclusion of the meal that thanks God for the food we have eaten.

Birkat Kohanim The "Priestly Blessing," a blessing from Numbers 6:24-26, which asks for God's blessing, protection, and peace.

Elijah A biblical prophet considered to be the forerunner of the Messianic Age, the messenger of the covenant, thought to be a protector of young children.

Hiddur mitzvah Literally "enhancing of mitzvah;" a Jewish principle whereby a *mitzvah* is embellished and beautified.

Kvatter, kvatterin Translated as "godfather" and "godmother"; both are assigned special roles in the *Berit Milah* and *Berit Bat* ceremonies.

Mohel, Mohelet, Mohalim, Mohelot — The person who performs a ritual circumcision.

Sandak — Literally understood as "helper of the child"; a designated individual who, traditionally, has the role of holding the baby as he is being circumcised.

Seudat mitzvah — A festive meal that enhances happy occasions and holidays.

Wimple — A binder for the Torah scroll.

OPENING
(5 minutes)

1. Invite the students to raise their hands if they belong to a team or club.
2. Ask those who raise their hands to tell what occurred when they first joined the team or club. Was there some kind of initiation or welcoming?
3. Encourage all the students to suggest ways in which one might be introduced and initiated into a new club or group. [a pledge of loyalty, participating in a welcome ceremony or party, receiving a special badge or uniform, being designated a locker or mailbox, etc.]
4. Write these suggestions on the board.
5. Explain to the students that they are now going to explore how babies and adults who choose Judaism get "initiated" or welcomed into the Jewish people. For babies, it is called a berit ceremony. For those who are choosing Judaism, it is called a conversion ceremony. In both instances the individual is welcomed into the covenant of Judaism.
6. Refer back to the list the students made at the beginning of this exercise. Explain that, like the list on the board, there are a number of specific rituals and documents that are

associated with being a new member of the Jewish people.

CLASSROOM ACTIVITIES

UNDERSTANDING OUR STORY
(10 minutes)

Materials: Writing paper and pencils.

1. Have the students read the "For the Sake of the Children" story on page 22 of the textbook.
2. Ask the students what it means to guarantee something.
3. Ask them to define "guarantor" based on the story.
4. Ask the students to think for a few moments about what they could do when they grow up to ensure that their children will learn about the importance of Torah and thus become the new guarantors.
5. Ask the students to consider the ways in which their own parents and grandparents have been guarantors for them.
6. Encourage the students to share their thoughts and/or record them in their journals.

BLESSING FOR THE MOMENT OF BIRTH
(15 minutes)

Materials: Copies of pages 109-110 from *On the Doorposts of Your House*.

1. Explain to students that while Jewish tradition offers us blessings and rituals for so many occasions and significant moments, there is no specific blessing to say at the moment of birth. The book *On the Doorposts of Your House*, published by the rabbinic organization of the Reform movement, suggests two different berachot.
2. Group the students into pairs and distribute copies of the two prayers.
3. Ask each pair to compare and contrast the

two suggestions. Which do they like better? Why?

4. Invite each pair to create their own suggested blessing for the miracle of birth.

5. Instruct the students to record their ideas in their family albums.

6. The students who are willing to share their blessings can read them to the class.

BRINGING BABY HOME
(15 minutes)

Materials: Writing paper and pencils.

1. Place the students in small work groups.

2. Instruct each group to develop a ritual for bringing a baby home for the first time. For reference, students can examine the naming ceremony (chapter 2 of the textbook), the *berit* ceremony (pp.29-30 of the textbook), and the blessing of a child on *erev* Shabbat (see Resources). The students can then create their own "new" ceremony.

3. Invite each group to role-play their ceremony for their classmates.

BERIT CEREMONIES
(20 minutes)

Material: Writing paper and pencils.

1. Divide the class into two groups.

2. Instruct each group to read the Focus sections "What is a *Berit*?", "*Berit Milah*—A Welcoming Ceremony for Boys," and "*Berit Bat*—A Welcoming Ceremony for Girls," on pages 24-27 and Life-Cycle Blessings on page 31 of the textbook (omitting the Text Study section). Then each group should read the section "The *Berit* Ceremony" on page 29 of the textbook.

3. One group should make a list of the components of a *Berit Bat* ceremony for girls while the other makes a list of the *Berit Milah* ceremony for boys.

4. Bring the two groups together.

5. Compare and contrast the two ceremonies, including the liturgy and rituals. What is the same in each ceremony? What is different?

6. Discuss the origins of the *Berit Bat* ceremony. Do the students think it fulfills the same purpose as *Berit Milah*? Do they have other suggestions for ways of entering girls into the covenant? Have them explain their answers.

THE HISTORY OF CIRCUMCISION
(10 minutes)

1. Have the students examine the first mention of *Berit Milah* in our people's history by reading the Text Study section on page 26 of the textbook.

2. Ask the students the following questions:
   - What is taking place here? [God is making a covenant with Abraham.]
   - What does God promise Abraham in the covenant? [many descendants, that he will be the father of royalty, wealth, land, good crops, an everlasting loyalty from God]

3. Instruct the students to continue reading the narrative at Genesis 17:9-14. What must Abraham do to enter into this covenant with God? [circumcise the skin of the foreskin on each male among them]. How will the covenant be maintained in future generations? [circumcision of the skin of the foreskin of each male at the age of eight days, or when required by the conversion process later in life]

4. Ask the students to suggest other ways in which people "mark" themselves physically. [Tattoos, piercing, etc.] Explain that while circumcision is a Jewish way of marking oneself, these other ways are currently not.

5. Ask the students to consider why it would have been important for Abraham to have a physical mark to represent the change he made in becoming a Jew.

CUSTOMS OF THE *BERIT* CEREMONY
(15 minutes)

1. Ask the students to share their own experiences with attending *Berit Bat* or *Berit Milah* ceremonies. Where were the ceremonies held, how did the room look, what symbolic objects were used, what followed the ceremony, etc. If no students can recall attending such a ceremony, the teacher can describe a personal experience.
2. Instruct the students to read the section "Customs of the *Berit* Ceremony" on page 28 of the textbook.
3. Review the term *hiddur mitzvah* and ask the students to recall some of the ways this *mitzvah* is observed in *berit* ceremonies as mentioned in the textbook.
4. Ask the students to list additional suggestions for *hiddur mitzvah* at *berit* ceremonies.
   Note: Alternatively, several parents could be invited in to speak to the class about the ceremonies they held for their children.

THE *BERIT* CEREMONY AND ITS BLESSINGS: A CLOSE-UP LOOK
(10 minutes)

1. Write the following blessing on the board:

   May you be blessed with children reared in health and well-being, devoted to Torah and to good deeds.

2. Ask the students to look at the photograph of a *berit* ceremony on page 29 of the textbook. What do they notice in the photograph? What objects are being used in the ceremony? Tell them that the mother and father who are holding the baby in the photo are using a family member's *talit* to wrap the baby. They are standing in front of their *chupah*, which is displayed on their living room wall. At the ceremony, they spoke about the blessing that was recited for them by the rabbi at their wedding. Refer to the blessing written on the board. Explain to the students that now the couple feels as though their wedding blessings are coming true!

3. Ask the students to read the section "The *Berit* Ceremony" on pages 29-30 of the textbook. Do the contents of the wedding blessing above sound familiar? [At the *berit* ceremony, after the *Kiddush* is recited, the *mohel, mohelet,* or rabbi blesses the baby with a special prayer wishing the baby a life of Torah study, good deeds, and a happy, lifelong marriage—found in the final paragraph of page 29 of the text.]

4. Compare the blessings and discuss the similarities and differences. Why would a blessing and a blessing used at a *berit* ceremony be similar?

WIMPLE MAKING
(20 minutes)

Materials: Rectangular pieces of cloth for each student; each piece should measure approximately five inches in width and at least four feet in length. Additionally, provide fabric paint and markers; materials for applique; stencil or illustrated samples of Jewish motifs and borders; samples of Hebrew print and calligraphy.

1. Explain to the students that wimples are traditionally Torah binders made of fabric that has been used to swaddle babies at birth.
2. Explain that the students may use these wimples at any special occasion in which they are involved and in which the Torah is being read or blessed by them. They may use them, for example, upon becoming *be'nei mitzvah* or at the *aufruf* before their marriage.
3. Print for the students the phrase "*Kisheym shenichnas labrit, keyn yichanes l'Torah, l'chupah, u'lema'asim tovim*—As he [she] has entered the covenant, so may he [she] be

28

brought to Torah, to the marriage canopy, and to good deeds." This is the traditional phrase found on Torah wimples. The students may instead wish to print something original or simply their Hebrew and English names. For reference and for some examples of wimples, consult the *Encyclopaedia Judaica*.

4. Distribute the materials and begin the art project.

5. Exhibit the wimples in a prominent place, with cards made by the students to explain what a wimple is.

CONVERSION—ANOTHER WAY OF JOINING THE JEWISH COMMUNITY

(**30 minutes:** 5 minutes to read the section of text; 5 minutes to prepare the questions; and 20 minutes for class discussion with guests)

Materials: Writing paper and pencils.

1. After the students have read the section, *"Conversion—Another Way of Joining the Jewish Community"* on pages 32-33 of the textbook, have them work as a class to develop questions to ask of someone who chose to become Jewish. Try to lead the students to questions of a nonpersonal nature such as: How long did it take? What were the requirements? Who taught you? What did you learn? What was the ceremony like?

2. Instruct the students to write down their questions.

3. Invite one or two Jews-by-Choice (perhaps parents of students) to visit the class so the students may interview them. If you are unsure how to go about finding possible guests, enlist the help of the rabbi.

4. When the guests visit the class, begin by asking each of them to introduce themselves.

5. Invite the students to ask their questions one at a time, allowing each student to ask at least one question.

6. Leave time at the end for any other information that the guests wish to add to the discussion.

ELIJAH THE PROPHET
(15 minutes)

Materials: Text of song "Eliyahu Hanavi."

1. Explain that traditionally the prophet Elijah is known as the one who will bring peace to the world and who will receive parents to children. Elijah is thought to be present at the Passover seder and at berit ceremonies.

2. Teach the song "Elijah Hanavi" and discuss the times when this song is sung (*Havdalah*, Pesach).

3. Ask the students to think about commonalities between *Havdalah*, Pesach, and the berit ceremonies. Why do we invoke Elijah the Prophet at each of these three times? [At all three we petition God for a peaceful future; at *Havdalah* for the coming week, at Pesach for the coming year, and at the berit ceremony for the lifetime of the new baby.]

PIDYON HABEN DEBATE
(20 minutes)

1. Write the phrase *Pidyon Haben* on the board.

2. Explain to the students that the textbook teaches us that Reform Jews do not observe the *Pidyon Haben* ceremony because it is only for boys.

3. Together, carefully read the Focus section *"Pidyon Haben—Redemption of the Firstborn"* on page 32 of the textbook.

4. Ask the students to list the features of the *Pidyon Haben* ceremony including its purpose. What other features of the Pidyon Haben ceremony might cause it to be less appealing to Reform Jews? [It distinguishes the firstborn; its purpose is to redeem the child from a lifetime of service in the ancient Temple—which doesn't exist anymore—and it

places emphasis on birth children, excluding adopted babies.]

5. Divide the class into two groups. Ask each group to imagine themselves as parents trying to decide whether or not to observe the *Pidyon Haben*. Each group should discuss why they might want to observe *Pidyon Haben* and why they might not.

6. Assign one group to be in favor of *Pidyon Haben* and the other to be against.

7. Invite each group to state their case, either pro or con. Then allow each group to respond to the other group's case. Finally, let each group defend their own position.

CHAPTER REVIEW

(5 minutes)

1. Write the titles "*Berit Milah*," "*Berit Bat*," and "Conversion Ceremony" on the board.

2. Ask the students to itemize the ritual objects and other items that would be needed to officiate at each of the ceremonies.

3. List the things under the name of each ceremony. (Students should use their texts for this exercise.)

4. Invite the students to compare and comment on the similarities and differences in the three *berit* ceremonies.

5. This review may be supplemented by bringing in different examples of these items for the students to look at.

CLOSURE

(5 minutes)

1. Ask the students to recall the terms and concepts associated with the life-cycle stage.

2. Add them to "The Jewish Life Cycle" diagram.

3. Assign a Family Enrichment activity.

4. Explain that the class has now learned how babies and Jews-by-Choice are welcomed into the Jewish community. In the upcoming segment, they will learn how children deepen their connection to Judaism, Jewish learning, and the Jewish community.

JOURNAL ASSIGNMENT

Ask students to write a paragraph on the meaning of *berit* ceremony.

FAMILY ENRICHMENT

BERIT CEREMONIES IN MY FAMILY

1. Hand out set of questions from appendix sheet 4 (p. 81).

2. When the students return with their answers, instruct the students to put the sheets in their family album.

YOU ARE THE TEACHER

1. Imagine that your family has been asked by the rabbi to tutor another family that wants to convert to Judaism.

2. Make a list of the essential things you would want to teach your "students."

3. Discuss why you chose each item on the list.

RESOURCES

Barth, Lewis, ed. *Berit Milah in the Reform Context*. Brit Milah Board of Reform Judaism. New York: UAHC Press, 1990.

Diamant, Anita. *The New Jewish Baby Book: Names, Ceremonies, and Customs for Today's Families*. Woodstock: Jewish Lights Publishing, 1993.

Einstein, Stephen J., and Lydia Kukoff, with Lisa Edwards, Marjorie Slome, and Hara Person. *Introduction to Judaism: A Source Book*. New York: UAHC Press, 1998.

Epstein, Lawrence. *Conversion to Judaism: A Guidebook*. Northvale, New Jersey: Jason Aronson, Inc., 1994.

Kukoff, Lydia. *Choosing Judaism*. New York: UAHC Press, 1981.

Stern, Chaim, ed. *On the Doorposts of Your House*. New York: CCAR, 1994.

Entering Religious School

CHAPTER SUMMARY

This chapter explores the ceremony of consecration, which takes place when students begin their formal Jewish studies. The value of lifelong Jewish study and learning is stressed in the Text Study and stories.

INSTRUCTIONAL OBJECTIVES

1. Explore the ceremony of consecration.
2. Study the *Ve'ahavta* prayer and examine the emphasis placed on teaching children.
3. Experience being a teacher.
4. Learn about Hillel, a rabbinic sage, and some of his important teachings.
5. Study the *Shema*, *Kiddush*, and *Hamotzi*, central prayers in Jewish life.

KEY TERMS

Bimah The Hebrew word for "raised platform," the place from which the Torah is read and the rabbi and cantor lead the services.

Birkat Kohanim The biblical "Priestly Blessing" from Numbers 6:24-26.

Consecration The ceremony that celebrates the beginning of a child's formal Jewish education.

Hakafot Literally, "processions;" refers to the parade around the sanctuary with the Torah, symbolizing that the Torah belongs to all the Jews of the community.

Matok The Hebrew word for "sweet."

Shul The Yiddish word for "synagogue."

Simcha A happy occasion.

Simchat Torah The Jewish festival that celebrates the giving of the Torah at Mount Sinai.

Talmud Torah Literally, "the study of Torah," a ritual mitzvah.

OPENING 1
(10 minutes)

Materials: Folded index cards or small pieces of folded paper (one for each student); bag of sweets with one for each student.

1. Before the students enter the classroom, write the phrase "Talmud Torah" in large clear letters in the middle of the board.
2. As the students enter the classroom, hand each one a folded index card or a folded slip of paper with the name of one candy or sweet food item on each (e.g., M&M's, Honey, Sugar, Chocolate Kisses, Good & Plenty, Reeses Pieces, Maple Syrup, Jelly, Molasses, Lollypops).

3. Instruct the students to keep the card or paper closed until all are seated and have heard the instructions.

4. When all the students are present, instruct them to open their cards and, without speaking, come as a group to the board, write their word any place on the board, and then return to their seats.

5. When everyone is seated once again, ask the students, "Who knows the common feature of all the words on the board?" [All of these things are sweet.]

6. Explain to the class that it is no mistake that sweet things surround the study of Torah. Studying Torah is such a rewarding and delightful experience! And when you find the time and opportunity to study and learn Torah with others, it is a real treat. There is, in fact, a long-standing tradition in Judaism to attract children to the study of Torah with sweets.

7. Give each student a real sweet to eat.

8. Tell the students that they will continue with a story that illustrates this tradition.

9. Continue with Classroom Activities.

OPENING 2
(15 minutes)

Materials: *Siddurim* or photocopies of the *Shema* and *Ve'ahavta* prayers.

1. Hand each student a *siddur* or a sheet of paper on which the *Shema* and *Ve'ahavta* prayers are copied but untitled. If the students are using the siddur, be prepared with the page number on which the *Shema* and *Ve'ahavta* prayers can be found. Announce only the page; do not state the names of the prayers.

2. Ask the students if they can identify the two prayers on the page.

3. Invite someone to lead the class in reciting the second part of the prayer.

4. Chant or speak the prayer aloud as a class.

5. After the recitation of the prayer, have the students list themes that emerge in these two pieces of liturgy.

6. Explain to the class that today's lesson will focus on a life-cycle ritual that developed from a theme in the *Ve'ahavta* prayer. Judaism considers teaching and passing on of Jewish values and traditions so important that there is an extensive body of legal literature pertaining to the teaching of Jewish children. And naturally, when Jewish children commence their studies, a joyous ritual is observed: the ceremony of consecration.

CLASSROOM ACTIVITIES

UNDERSTANDING OUR STORY
(10 minutes)

1. Ask the students to define the word incentive. (You may need to use it in a sentence for the students to remember what it means, i.e., the promise of something that causes one to move to action.)

2. Tell the students that they will be reading a story about a young boy who needed a little incentive to begin his Jewish studies.

3. Have the students read the story "As Sweet As Honey" on pages 36-37 of the textbook.

4. Ask the students if they have ever needed a little extra incentive to do something they were reluctant to do. For those who answer in the affirmative ask: What was that incentive? Did it work? Why or why not?

5. Ask the students if they think the method used in the story is a good one. Why? Why not?

FOCUS: THE TORAH—
WHERE JEWISH LEARNING BEGINS
(15 minutes)

Materials: Words to Etz Chayim Hi.

1. After reading together the Focus section "The Torah—Where Jewish Learning Begins" on page 38 of the textbook, tell the students that it is said that the Torah is like the tree of life itself.

2. Ask the students to explain this analogy.

3. Discuss the traditional explanations: that as we mature and/or as time passes, things that may have been confusing at first become better understood. This rule of life is just as true with the study of Torah. The reading of Torah is a constant cycle. We repeat the cycle of readings every new year, and like the tree of life, we gain branches of understanding and beauty we didn't know were possible.

4. Direct the students in a dialogue about their own understanding of Proverbs 3:18. Ask them to discuss how Torah has been a tree of life for them or others they know.

5. Ask the students to discuss why they think Judaism considers life-long Torah study to be so critical to Jewish life.

6. Invite the cantor or music specialist in to teach the class the text and music to *Etz Chayim Hi*. (Consult Transcontinental Music for resources.)

ART ACTIVITY: COLLAGE
(15 minutes)

Materials: Mural paper; glue; old magazines; scissors; markers.

1. In black marker on the mural paper, write the words to Proverbs 3:18 from page 38 of the textbook.

2. Group the students into pairs.

3. Provide each pair with materials.

4. Ask the students to create an artistic representation of Proverbs 3:18. How can they show what the words mean?

5. After the class is done with the project, ask the students to be seated and discuss the mural.

BEFORE YOU BEGIN YOUR FORMAL JEWISH EDUCATION
(15 minutes)

1. Have the students read the section "Before You Begin Your Formal Jewish Education" on pages 38-39 of the textbook.

2. Assign each student a partner.

3. Ask the pairs to think of a memorable Jewish experience or celebration. The students should relate their experiences to their partners, providing as much detail as possible.

4. Give the pairs a time limit of 60 seconds. After 60 seconds, the "listeners" will recite the details of their partners' stories to the rest of the class.

5. Repeat the process with the roles reversed.

6. As a class, discuss the impact of these early memories on the student's Jewish education. Did the experiences make them want more Jewish education? Why or why not?

7. Ask the students to explore the relationship between their Jewish experiences and their formal Jewish education. How did the early experiences lay the ground for their Jewish studies?

TEXT STUDY
(15 minutes)

1. Ask the students to list, as a group, what takes place at the Passover seder.

2. Record their answers on the board. [Possible answers: We eat a big fancy meal, tell the story of our ancestors' exodus from Egypt, sing songs, look for a hidden piece of *matzah*, eat *matzah*, etc.]

3. Ask the students why they think this ritual is repeated year after year. [Tradition commands us to observe the festival of Pesach and to retell the story of the Exodus each year.]

4. Proceed by having the students read the Text Study section on page 39 of the textbook.

5. Explain any parts of the text from Deuteronomy 6:20-25 for which the students may need clarification.

6. Invite the students to write a paragraph or a poem about the cyclical nature of Jewish holidays and celebrations.

FOCUS: THE JEWISH VIEW OF EDUCATION
(30 minutes)

Materials: A list of the religious school's overall curriculum on a sheet of chart paper; writing paper and pencils.

1. In preparation for this activity, obtain a copy of the synagogue's religious school curriculum from the director of education or the Rabbi.

2. List all the areas of study that are covered in the overall curriculum on a sheet of chart paper. [Torah, holidays, life cycle, Israel, etc.]

3. Have the chart paper rolled up and ready to show the class.

4. Ask the students to read the section "The Jewish View of Education" on page 40 of the textbook.

5. Working in groups of two or three, have the students make a list of all the topics and skills they have studied in religious school thus far. Then have them list the things they have learned from living in a Jewish home.

6. Ask the groups to report their lists, and to record their responses on chart paper. Then ask the students to try to imagine what they will study and what they hope to study in the years to come as they continue their Jewish education.

7. When the students have listed all their answers, hang the chart paper on which the school's curriculum is recorded.

8. Have students compare their list with the actual school curriculum. What is the same? What is different?

9. Together, brainstorm all the ways that they can "complement" their formal religious school studies in order to cover all the areas of Jewish learning that they have listed.

10. Discuss with the students any gaps they may perceive in the list of the religious school curriculum. Are there Jewish experiences that have been important to them (camp, retreats, youth group, nursery school, field trips) that they feel should be on the list? Explain.

ENTERING RELIGIOUS SCHOOL
(20 minutes)

Materials: Writing paper and pencils.

1. Have the students read the sections "Entering Religious School" and "The Consecration Ceremony" on pages 41-43 of the textbook.

2. Ask the students if they remember their own consecration into religious school. From those who answer in the affirmative, make a list of the details they remember.

3. Ask the students what other activities, rituals, prayers, blessings, etc. would make a meaningful consecration ceremony.

4. Divide the students into groups of three or four to craft a ceremony of consecration. Allow time for groups to present their ceremonies to the rest of the class.

5. Invite the students to write a letter to the rabbi or the education committee with some of their suggestions.

HILLEL ON THE ROOF
(20 minutes)

1. Write the following sayings on the board:
   - In a place where there are no human beings, try to be one.
   - Don't judge your fellow human being until you have reached that person's place.
   - If I am not for myself, who will be for me? If I am only for myself, then what am I? If not now, when?

- Love peace and pursue it; love people and bring them to Torah.

2. Have the students read the passage "Hillel on the Roof" on page 41 of the textbook.

3. Present the above teachings by Hillel, and have groups of students create skits that embody the sayings on the board. The students should also use the actual saying some place in the play.

4. Invite each group to present their dramatizations of Hillel's teachings to the entire class.

5. If time permits, discuss each of the teachings.

6. Ask the students to select one statement that best describes their own attitude toward Jewish life. Have them explain their selection.

FOCUS:
THE CONSECRATION CEREMONY
(20 minutes)

Materials: Torah scroll.

1. Arrange for the students to visit the sanctuary to see the Torah up close.

2. After entering the sanctuary, ask the students to look around and see if there are any symbols used that have to do with the idea of Torah as a tree of life.

3. Ask the students to read the Focus Section "The Consecration Ceremony" on pages 42-43 of the textbook.

4. Open the Torah and have the students look inside. Are there any symbols associated with the Torah itself that have to do with Torah as the tree of life?

5. Roll the scroll to Numbers 6 and read verses 24, 25, and 26. Ask the students to find familiar words in the scroll.

6. While you are on the *bimah*, have the class review the words of the *Birkat Kohanim* in Hebrew and English, or have the rabbi or cantor do so. Explain how these words were originally used.

7. Ask the students to try to interpret the words

of the blessing. What hopes and aspirations does the blessing contain? If they themselves have ever been blessed with these words, ask them to describe their memories of how it felt.

8. When the students return to the classroom, have them record their impressions of this visit to the sanctuary in their family albums. Have them consider the atmosphere in the sanctuary and their own feelings of being in such close proximity to the Torah.

FOCUS:
THE CONSECRATION CEREMONY
(5 minutes)

1. Have the students look at the photo on page 43 of the textbook.

2. Ask them to suggest reasons why the two adults are holding the *talit* over the heads of the young students. Who might these adults be? Ask the students to consider why certain adults representing particular roles in the synagogue might be involved in the ceremony.

3. Who are the people who would be their figurative *talit* holders? Who are the people who they would want to bless them and sustains them in their Jewish studies?

LIFE-CYCLE BLESSINGS
(10 minutes)

Materials: *Kiddush* cup, grape juice, *challah*. Bring a *Kiddush* cup, some grape juice, and a *challah* to class.

1. After reviewing the life-cycle blessings on page 44 of the textbook, bless the grape juice and the *challah* and eat them in class.

2. Ask the students to suggest reasons why the *Shema*, *Kiddush*, and *Hamotzi* are central Jewish prayers. [*Shema*—declaration from Torah of a Jew's faith in One God. *Kiddush*—a celebratory blessing said at every happy occasion on festivals and at every Shabbat meal. *Hamotzi*—Bread sustains us, and so the

blessing for bread is like a blessing for that which keeps us alive.]

3. Why are these blessings and rituals normally part of life-cycle rituals?

JEWISH SONG
(10 minutes)

Materials: The text and perhaps a recording of the chosen song.

1. There are several Hebrew texts about the importance of Torah and education that are set to song. Bring examples of these texts from the list below and have the music specialist, cantor, rabbi, or volunteer parent teach them to the class.

2. If possible, have the students serve as a choir at Shabbat services to sing the songs they have learned.

It Is a Tree of Life to Them That Hold Fast to It— in Shireinu (Transcontinental Music, 1997)

Ve'ahavta—Michael Isaacson in *NFTY's Fifty* (Transcontinental Music)

And Thou Shalt Love—Debbie Friedman

THE MITZVAH OF TEACHING
(30 minutes)

1. Arrange for the class to "mentor" a group of younger students.

2. The following is a list of activities in which the fifth- or sixth-grade level of students should be able to engage with younger students:
   - Reading Jewish stories
   - Creating a picture frame with the primary student's Hebrew name
   - Reviewing the *aleph bet*
   - Playing Jewish trivia
   - Practicing blessings for Shabbat at home
   - Holiday rituals and blessings

3. After your class returns to its own classroom study, ask the students to write a few

sentences in their family albums about the experience of teaching younger students in the religious school.

CONSECRATION ADDRESS
(15 minutes)

Materials: Writing paper and pencils.

1. Ask the students what they recall, if anything, from their own consecration ceremonies.

2. Invite the students to imagine that they were being asked by the rabbi to address this year's consecration class during the ceremony. Ask the students to think seriously about what would they want to say to the new students. What sage advice would they pass on about religious school? About being Jewish? About growing up?

3. Instruct the students to write a consecration address.

4. When they have finished, ask the students to share their addresses.

5. You may choose to show the addresses to the rabbi or educator for possible use in next year's consecration ceremony.

CHAPTER REVIEW
(15 minutes)

1. Ask each student to say one new thing they learned about Jewish education.

2. Ask the students to name the prayers and blessings that are associated in this lesson with Jewish education.

3. Invite the students to explain why these prayers and blessings are connected to beginning one's Jewish education.

CLOSURE

1. Explain to the students that life presents us with many opportunities and challenges. As Jews, we are fortunate to have a guide for making decisions: Torah. Thus it is crucial for

us to begin Talmud Torah early on in life. When a child begins Torah study, it is considered so special that the consecration celebration was created to mark this sacred occasion.

2. Ask the students for suggestions of words and concepts connected to this life-cycle stage. Use these words and concepts to fill in another section of "The Jewish Life-Cycle" diagram.

3. Tell the students that consecration is not the only special ceremony centered around Jewish study. Next they will see that becoming bar/bat mitzvah entails Torah study on a deeper level and also gives the young person a chance to teach the congregation.

JOURNAL ASSIGNMENT

Ask students to write a paragraph describing what they remember from the time they began religious school.

FAMILY ENRICHMENT

NEW BEGINNINGS

1. Have the students create a page called "New Beginnings," in their family album.

2. With their parents and grandparents, have the students record the details of some of the memorable beginnings that have occurred in their lives thus far.

3. Where possible, have the students collect photographs and memorabilia that relate to the list.

4. The list can include beginning to walk, beginning preschool, beginning to read, beginning to write, beginning a sport, beginning a club, etc.

5. Where photographs are not available, the students can cut out pictures from a magazine, find images on the Internet, or draw illustrations.

6. Have the students bring their illustrations and their lists with explanations to class.

7. Instruct the students to add this material to their family album.

RESOURCES

Encyclopaedia Judaica. Jerusalem: Keter Publishing House, Jerusalem Ltd., 1972.

HaLevi, Aaron. *Sefer haHinnuch: The Book of Mitzvah Education*. Vol. 1. New York: Feldheim Publishers, 1978.

www.uahcweb.org/educate/parent/—for a Parent Page Newsletter (issue 1—Getting Started).

www.uahc.org—for resolution on Torah Study (1997).

Bar/Bat Mitzvah

CHAPTER SUMMARY

This chapter explores the important life-cycle ceremony that marks the transition to Jewish adulthood and full membership in the community, bar and bat mitzvah. The history and development of bar and bat mitzvah is detailed, as well as the typical elements of the modern celebration.

INSTRUCTIONAL OBJECTIVES

1. Explore the rites and responsibilities of Jewish adulthood.
2. Learn what it means to gain full membership into the Jewish community.
3. Study the first bat mitzvah ceremony and investigate why bat mitzvah has become an important ritual in Reform Jewish communities.

KEY TERMS

Aliyah　　Literally "going up"; one meaning is being called up to recite the Torah blessings.

Ba'al
Shem Tov　(1698-1760) The founder of modern Chasidism, his name literally means "Master of the Good Name." He was called this because of his uncanny abilities as a leader and a healer.

*Benei
mitzvah*　Plural form of *bar mitzvah*; literally, "children of the commandment."

Bar　　　Aramaic for "son"; the Hebrew is *ben*.

Bat　　　Hebrew for "daughter."

Berachah　Hebrew for "blessing."

Bimah　　Podium on which the service leaders and Torah readers stand.

*Birkat
Kohanim*　The "Priestly Blessing," a blessing from Numbers 6:24-26, which asks for God's blessing, protection, and peace.

Cantillation　The art of liturgical chanting. The cantillation notes (also known as trope) are symbols that represent musical phrases.

Chumash　A book that contains the Five Books of Moses and, in some instances, also brief commentary.

Haftarah　A reading from the biblical books of the Prophets that is assigned to correspond to the weekly Torah reading.

Hillel and
Shamma　Two rabbinic sages and adversaries. They often argued talmudic principles from opposite perspectives.

Maftir　　The last section of the Torah reading for the week; in many instances, this may be the section of the Torah that the *benei mitzvah* chant.

Minyan　　A quorum of ten adult Jews traditionally needed for certain types of communal worship.

CHAPTER FIVE

Pirke Avot A talmudic tractate devoted to ethical precepts.

Seudat mitzvah A festive meal that enhances happy occasions and holidays.

Shacharit The morning worship service.

OPENING
(5 minutes)

Materials: Copies of handout.

1. Hand the students a sheet of paper on which the following is written:
   - I know that I will be an adult when... because...
2. Ask the students to complete the statement individually and to be prepared to discuss their answer.
3. Invite the students to share their answers.
4. When all the students have had their turn, explain that today they will study the life-cycle stage of bar and bat mitzvah, the ceremony that celebrates a young Jew's transition to adulthood.

CLASSROOM ACTIVITIES

UNDERSTANDING OUR STORY
(15 minutes)

1. Have the students read the story "Two Tales of Becoming Bar Mitzvah" on pages 48-49 of the textbooks.
2. Instruct the students to note any words and phrases that are unfamiliar to them.
3. At the conclusion of the story, have the students discuss the possible meanings (found in Key Terms above) of these words and phrases.
4. Then have the students discuss the main teachings of this legend.
5. Ask the students to imagine why such a story might originally have been told and then pre-

served for many centuries. Have the students consider which aspects of this tale are still relevant. How is this story modern despite its age? How might you incorporate the lessons of this story into your own bar/bat mitzvah? How have others emulated the main point of this story? What does this story teach us is the essential aspect of bar/bat mitzvah?

THE BAR OR BAT MITZVAH CEREMONY
(30 minutes)

Materials: Art supplies and construction paper; additional resources.

1. Divide the students into pairs to read the Focus section "How Bar and Bat Mitzvah Developed" on page 50 of the textbook.
2. Hand each group a sheet of large construction paper.
3. Instruct the students to draw a diagonal line from one corner of the top of the page to the opposite corner at the bottom of the page.
4. Based on what they have read, ask the pairs to depict an early bar mitzvah ceremony in one half of the page. If available, have the students consult other resources such as those listed at the end of this chapter.
5. As a class, have the students read the second Focus section in this chapter, "The Bar or Bat Mitzvah Ceremony" on pages 53-54 of the textbook.
6. Have the students work again with their partner to complete the artwork.
7. Instruct them now to draw, on the other half of the page, a modern-day bar or bat mitzvah ceremony.
8. Ask each group to present their illustrations.
9. Together, discuss the similarities, differences, and developments of the bar/bat mitzvah ceremony from the sixth to the twentieth centuries. Ask the students to consider the following questions: What elements have been preserved in the bar/bat mitzvah ceremony?

Are there things that have been lost that should be reinstituted? Are there modern developments that should be eliminated? Finally, have the students create a title for their artwork and display the drawings in the classroom.

THE FIRST BAT MITZVAH
(15 minutes)

1. Have the students read the section "The First Bat Mitzvah" on page 51 of the textbook.
2. Ask the students to respond to the following questions:
   - What feelings did Judith Kaplan Eisenstein experience as the first girl to celebrate becoming bat mitzvah?
   - Why do you think Judith agreed to become bat mitzvah even though she was so worried about what people would think?
   - In your experience and from the reading, how do you think bat mitzvah ceremonies today differ from the one Judith describes?
   - In your own words, state why bat mitzvah was an important Jewish innovation.
   - What are other modern Jewish innovations that you know of?
   - In the middle of the fourth paragraph of her story, Judith describes the bat mitzvah as an ordeal. What's an ordeal? Describe a time when you experienced an ordeal. What were you feeling? How did it end? Was it a positive or negative experience?

WHY BECOMING BAR OR BAT MITZVAH IS IMPORTANT
(10 minutes)

1. Have the students read the section "Why Becoming Bar or Bat Mitzvah Is Important" on page 52 of the textbook.

2. Ask the students to complete one of the following in a paragraph:
   - Becoming bar or bat mitzvah is important to me because_____
   - It is important for all young Jewish people to become *benei mitzvah* because_____
   - Have the students share what they have written.
   - Seal their responses in preaddressed envelopes.
   - Ask the religious school principal to save the envelopes and mail them to the students during their bar/bat mitzvah year.

A TORAH IS WRITTEN
(20 minutes)
Materials: *A Torah Is Written* by Paul Cowan (Philadelphia: Jewish Publication Society, 1986).

1. Ask the class what they know about how a Torah is written. Pose some questions that are answered by the text. What other questions do they have about the process?
2. Read the class Paul Cowan's *A Torah Is Written*, and show them the accompanying photographs.
3. Allow for questions and comments as you read.
4. If there are other questions the students have that are not answered by the book, ask the rabbi or educator.
5. If possible, arrange for a scribe to come visit the class and explain his or her work.

TEXT STUDY
(20 minutes)
Materials: Any props or costumes necessary for skits.

1. Divide the class into two groups.
2. Have each group study the texts from *Pirke Avot* on pages 52-53 of the textbook.
3. Explain who were Hillel and Shammai.

4. Assign one group the precepts from 1:14 and the other 1:15.

5. Each group should create a five-minute skit that dramatizes their precept and especially demonstrates the connection between the verse and becoming a bar/bat mitzvah.

6. Invite the groups to present their skits to each other.

7. In conclusion, have the students select the precept that best summarizes their own idea of bar/bat mitzvah.

8. Ask them to explain whether they would side with Hillel or Shammai, and why.

LIFE-CYCLE BLESSINGS
(20 minutes)

1. Review the *Birkat Kohanim* blessing found on page 54 of the textbook.

2. Ask students where they may have seen this blessing in a previous chapter. [The *berit* ceremony]

3. Ask students to suggest similarities in the two life-cycle stages. [Both are beginnings— the berit ceremony is the beginning of life; bar/bat mitzvah is the beginning of adulthood.]

4. Continue by looking at the blessings before and after the Torah reading on page 54 of the textbook.

5. If possible, lead the students in chanting the blessings.

6. Tell the students that there is a traditional blessing said by the father at his son's bar mitzvah ceremony in which the father says, *"Baruch sheptarani May'onsho shel zeh—* Blessed is the One who has freed me from the responsibility for this [child]." Clearly, the responsibility for living a life of *mitzvot* fell upon the young person when he reached the age of Jewish adulthood. Explain that most Reform synagogues have abandoned this practice. Ask the students why they think this might be the case. [The age of thirteen is no

longer considered adult. Many parents are not willing to allow their thirteen-year-old children to make their own decisions about their Jewish observances and about their ongoing Jewish learning.] Instead, many Reform congregations have a tradition in which one or both parents may come to the *bimah* and bless their son or daughter at this sacred moment. The content of these personal blessings varies; however, most parents state how they are proud of their child and how they wish a long, healthy, blessed, and Jewishly rich life for their child. Ask the students: How are the traditional father's blessing and the contemporary parental blessing of a child different? How are they similar?

7. Have the students write a blessing they would like their parents to give them at their own bar/bat mitzvah.

THE CELEBRATION
(15 minutes)

1. Ask the students to raise their hands if they have ever attended a bar or bat mitzvah celebration.

2. Call on those students who have raised their hands and ask them to recall details of the celebration. What did they like the most about the celebration, and why? What aspects of the celebration made it feel like a special Jewish celebration?

3. Have the students read the third Focus section, "The Celebration," on pages 56-57 of the textbook.

4. Ask students to write a short paragraph describing what they would plan (or are planning) for their own bar or bat mitzvah celebration, keeping in mind the ideals of our early rabbinic leaders and current movement sensibilities.

PANEL DISCUSSION
(15 minutes for question preparation, 20 minutes for the panel discussion)

1. Invite several students who have become bar/bat mitzvah in the previous year or two, as well as one or two adults who became bar/bat mitzvah recently.

2. Have the students prepare questions ahead of time. Ask them to think about what they would really like to know about the process. How did they prepare? How did they feel the day of the ceremony? What did they like the best? The least? Why was it important enough for the adult(s) to do at a later age?

3. Seat the guests at a table, and arrange the students on the other side.

4. Allow the students to take turns answering questions.

FAMILY INTERVIEWS
(15 minutes)

Materials: Writing paper and pencils.

1. Have the students work in pairs to create the first draft of an interview sheet for their parents, grandparents, and other relatives in order to question them about becoming bar or bat mitzvah.

2. Remind the students that some of the questions should explore how the experience felt and other questions should seek to find out practical information.

3. Urge the students to interview relatives from earlier generations in particular.

4. Allow class time for the students to share their findings.

5. Make suggestions about additional questions or help rephrase questions.

6. Ask the students to rewrite the interview sheet, incorporating changes.

7. Encourage students to bring in photos or ritual objects associated with the celebration they explored.

JEWISH ADULT BEHAVIOR
(20 minutes)

Materials: Handout entitled "Some Privileges and Responsibilities of Jewish Adults" from appendix sheet 5.

1. Prepare a handout in advance of class listing the adult privileges and responsibilities. You can use the list from appendix sheet 5 (p. 82).

2. Remind the students that becoming bar or bat mitzvah represents a change in one's status in the Jewish community. *Benei mitzvah* are considered to be adults and as such gain new privileges and responsibilities.

3. Ask the students to order the list from most challenging to least. Number one should be the item that they consider most challenging. Number twelve is the item that they consider least challenging.

4. After students have worked on their own list for ten minutes, ask them to share their responses and their reasoning with their classmates.

CHAPTER REVIEW

1. Ask each student to write down three new things they learned about becoming bar or bat mitzvah from the study of this chapter.

2. Draw a line down the board, and label one side "challenges" and the other side "rewards."

3. Have the students create lists of the rewards and challenges associated with becoming bar/bat mitzvah from the material they read, and record their suggestions under the respective headings.

CLOSURE

1. Have the students read the sections "Life after Bar and Bat Mitzvah" and "Summary" on page 57 of the textbook.

2. Stress the fact that becoming *benei mitzvah*

will mark a new beginning that carries with it many new responsibilities and privileges.

3. Remind the students that one of Judaism's highest ideals is perpetual learning.

4. Ask the students for suggestions of terms and concepts related to this life-cycle stage to add to "The Jewish Life Cycle" diagram.

5. Tell the students that the next chapter will explore a formal learning opportunity for young people a couple of years after they reach the milestone of becoming *benei mitzvah*.

JOURNAL ASSIGNMENT

Ask students to write a paragraph describing how they feel about becoming bar/bat mitzvah someday.

FAMILY ENRICHMENT

BAR/BAT MITZVAH AS A TIME OF CHANGE

Materials: Copy of Genesis 32:25-31.

1. Explain in a cover letter to the families of your students that becoming bar or bat mitzvah shows the world that a young person has changed from a Jewish child to a Jewish adult. This change does not happen overnight. To truly become a Jewish adult, one must master many skills and learn many things.

2. Send the students home with an assignment to read a special biblical text with their parents: Genesis 32:25-31. Provide a photocopy of these verses. Explain that it is the narrative in which Jacob undergoes a significant change

on his way to becoming a Jewish adult.

3. Ask the family to discuss the questions on appendix sheet 6 (p. 83) after reading the biblical selection.

4. Instruct the students to add the material to their family album.

TZEDAKAH AND THE FAMILY

1. Send the students home with the quotations about tzedakah on appendix sheet 7 (p. 84).

2. Families are to first study and discuss these quotes and then develop goals for giving tzedakah as a family.

3. Ask the students to report on their family discussions. What goals did they set? How did they arrive at those conclusions?

4. Instruct the students to add the material to their family album.

RESOURCES

Binder Kadden, Barbara, and Bruce Kadden. *Teaching Jewish Life Cycles: Traditions and Activities*. Denver, CO.: A.R.E. Publications, 1997.

Marder, Janet. "When Bar/Bat Mitzvah Loses Meaning," from *Reform Judaism*, vol. 21, no. 2 (Winter, 1992).

Salkin, Jeffrey K. *Putting God on the Guest List: How to Reclaim the Spiritual Meaning of Your Child's Bar or Bat Mitzvah*. Woodstock, Vt.: Jewish Lights Publishing, 1992.

Siegel, Danny. "Bar/Bat Mitzvah Heroes," from *Reform Judaism*, vol. 21, no. 2 (Winter, 1992).

"Elana's Gift," from *Reform Judaism*, vol. 21, no. 2 (Winter, 1992).

Confirmation

CHAPTER SUMMARY

This chapter explores the history and current customs associated with the life-cycle ceremony of confirmation. Confirmation is stressed as an affirmation of lifelong Jewish learning and involvement in the Jewish community.

INSTRUCTIONAL OBJECTIVES

1. Examine past and current confirmation ceremonies in the Reform Jewish community.
2. Learn about the connection between the holiday of Shavuot and the ceremony of confirmation.

KEY TERMS

Confirmands	young people participating in a confirmation program.
Confirmation	A conscious affirmation or acknowledgment; a ceremony held on or near the holiday of Shavuot in which high school students affirm their connection and devotion to Judaism.
Gemilut chasadim	Acts of loving-kindness.
Mishnah	Compiled and edited in approximately 200 C.E. the *Mishnah* groups the laws in Torah thematically and provides additional rabbinic legislation and commentary.
Shavuot	The holiday that celebrates the giving of the Torah and its acceptance by the Jewish people at Mount Sinai.
Talmud	A text that expands upon and explains the *Mishnah*. This rabbinic commentary is also known as *Gemara*.

OPENING
(10 minutes)

Materials: Copies of survey "What Does Jewish Tradition Teach Us about Religious Education?" from appendix sheet 8.

1. As students enter the classroom, hand them the survey "What Does Jewish Tradition Teach Us about Religious Education?" from appendix sheet 8 (p. 85).
2. Instruct them to take a few moments to fill in the answers. What do they think Jewish tradition teaches us about these stages in a Jewish child's religious education?
3. When the students have finished writing, invite them to share their ideas.
4. Then ask the students to name the celebrations associated with these same ages [e.g.: age five = consecration, age thirteen = bar/bat mitzvah]. Explain to the students that this class session will explore the last stage mentioned in the survey.
5. Explain to the students that the life-cycle stage of confirmation, which occurs during the high

45

school years, is about commitment to ongoing Jewish study and learning.

6. Save the completed surveys for use in the Classroom Activity "Jewish Study" on page 47.

CLASSROOM ACTIVITIES

UNDERSTANDING OUR STORY
(10 minutes)

1. Have the students read the story "The Inheritance" on pages 60-61 of the textbook.

2. Ask the students the following questions:
   - In the second paragraph of the story, how did the daughter feel when she first saw and held the jewel?
   - Why do you think that the jewel seemed to feel alive?
   - What does this story teach us about Judaism?
   - What aspects of Judaism does the opal represent?
   - What opals have been given to you? What instructions came with your jewel? What instructions will you pass on?
   - What do you think would have happened in the story if instructions had been added by each generation? What instructions have you added to your own Jewish life?

CONFIRMATION—A NEW JEWISH LIFE-CYCLE CEREMONY
(10 minutes)

1. Have the students read the Focus section "Confirmation—A New Jewish Life-Cycle Ceremony" on page 62 of the textbook.

2. Ask the students to explain in their own words the origin of the confirmation ceremony. [They were substitutions for bar mitzvah ceremonies.]

3. Ask the students to consider the question of why Reform Jews today continue the practice of confirmation, even after bar and then bat mitzvah has been reintroduced into the life cycle. [Confirmation has taken on a special meaning, making it more than just a substitute for bar/bat mitzvah.]

4. Write the following categories on the board: Origin, Meaning, Rituals, Liturgy, Education.

5. Using these categories, have the students compare bar/bat mitzvah with confirmation. Discuss the differences and similarities. Debate the merits of each ceremony.

6. Ask the students whether they think Reform Jews need both bar/bat mitzvah and confirmation.

TEXT STUDY
(15 minutes)

Materials: Markers; blank sheets of paper; twenty feet of clothesline (cord or string); clothespins.

1. Suspend a long cord or string from one end of the classroom to the other, as though it were a clothesline.

2. Explain to the students that the Ten Commandments are often used to symbolize all of the laws of Torah. As the first ten laws given to the Jewish people at Mount Sinai, they were the basis of all the other commandments.

3. Ask the students to recall as many of the Ten Commandments as possible.

4. Ask for volunteers to write each commandment in large letters with a marker on a piece of paper, one commandment per piece of paper. Each commandment should be written down only once. Help the students to remember commandments, if necessary.

5. Place the students in a group, and give them the ten pieces of paper.

6. Instruct them to work together to put the commandments in the right order.

7. When they think the commandments are in the correct order, invite the students to attach

the commandments to the line with clothes-pins.

8. When they are done, invite them to compare their list to the list on page 63 of the text-book. If necessary, allow them to adjust the order on the clothesline.

THE ELEVENTH COMMANDMENT
(15 minutes)

Materials: Paper and pencils; art supplies.

1. Ask the students to review the Ten Commandments on page 63 of the textbook. Remind them that throughout their study of the Jewish life cycle they have encountered innovations (like confirmation).
2. Instruct them to take a piece of blank paper and write a suggestion for an eleventh commandment. Their suggestion should be based on their own feelings, their sensibilities regarding the world in which we live, and their concerns for our society.
3. Collect the responses, and read them aloud to the class.
4. If time permits, allow the students to decorate their suggestions and post their artwork around the classroom.

WE WERE THERE
(30 minutes)

Materials: Copies of Exodus text; poems or stories related to Mount Sinai experience; costumes and props; paper and pencils.

1. Tell the class that Jewish tradition teaches us that all the Jewish people, past, present, and future (even those who were not yet born, and all the people who would eventually choose Judaism), were at Mount Sinai when the Torah was given by God to the entire Jewish community. According to this, then, every one of us was there, too.
2. Allow the students to choose one of the following two activities: either a dramatic

presentation or a creative writing exercise. Divide the class into two groups according to the students' choices.
3. Instruct each group to read the section from the Torah describing the events at Mount Sinai (Exodus 19:16-20:15).
4. The group that selected drama will reenact the events based upon the text, incorporating any other *midrash*, story, or poem about Mount Sinai that you can find for them. They may use props and costumes and other available materials. Urge creativity.
5. The writing group will write a collaborative story based on the Exodus. A sheet of paper will be passed from person to person. The paper will be folded in such a way that students are able to see only the last line of the previous paragraph. Each student will read that last line to him- or herself and continue with his or her new paragraph, adding to the existing story. Begin the collaborative story with the following paragraph: "It all began with a great clap of thunder. The Israelites were fast asleep in their tents. Then there was total confusion in the camp. Children and babies were crying, men and women were running this way and that, trying to make sense of the noise and chaos." Remind the students that their story is about the events at Mount Sinai (in other words, keep them focused).
6. When both groups are finished, invite them to make presentations to the other group.

JEWISH STUDY
(10 minutes)

Materials: Copies of *Pirke Avot*; completed surveys (from Opening activity, p. 45).

1. Explain to the students that one of the highest ideals in Jewish life is ongoing study and learning.
2. Tell the students that Jewish teachers have been thinking about how to design a lifelong

Jewish education for many centuries. From approximately the year 300 C.E. we find the following instructions for Jewish education:

> [Rabbi Judah ben Tema] used to say: "At five [one begins the study of] the Bible. At ten the *Mishnah*. At thirteen [one takes on] the [responsibility for] the *mitzvot*. At fifteen [one begins the study of] the Talmud." (*Pirke Avot* 5:21)

3. Write the above text on the board.
4. Clarify for the students any terms that may be unclear.
5. Distribute the survey on Jewish education that the students completed during the Opening activity.
6. Using these surveys as well as the selection from *Pirke Avot*, have the class write a modern equivalent of Ben Tema's recommendations. Invite the students to add as many ages as they wish.
7. Post Ben Tema's words along with those of the students in the classroom.

EXTRA, EXTRA, READ ALL ABOUT IT
(20 minutes)

Materials: Handouts with headlines; writing paper and pencils.

Have the students read the Torah narrative describing the event at Sinai (Exodus 19:16-20:15).

1. Print the following newspaper headlines on the blackboard:
   - GREAT LIGHTNING AND THUNDER ACCOMPANY JEWS RECEIVING TORAH AT SINAI!
   - SOME SAY 10 TOO MANY!! SOME SAY 10 ARE TOO FEW!!
   - "WE WILL DO AND WE WILL HEAR," JEWS REPLY UPON RECEIVING TORAH FROM GOD!
2. Ask the students to write an article based on their choice of one of the suggested head-

lines. Their articles should contain some "newsworthy" details as well as some imagined "personal" accounts of the experience of receiving and accepting the Torah.
3. After ten to fifteen minutes of writing, the students should be invited to share their stories.

OUR SYNAGOGUE'S HISTORY OF CONFIRMATION
(20 minutes)

1. If your synagogue has a long history of confirmation, there are probably years of confirmation class photographs hanging on wall somewhere in the synagogue.
2. Take the students on a field trip to see the photographs.
3. Standing near the photographs, ask the students to find the earliest photograph.
4. Ask the students to study the photographs and determine what about confirmation has changed through the years as seen in the photographs. What has stayed the same? Ask the students if they can explain any of the changes.
5. Ask the students to think about what having these photographs teaches them about Reform Jewish history and about the history of the congregation.

CONFIRMATION AND SHAVUOT
(20 minutes)

Materials: Copies of Torah texts; writing paper and pencils.

1. Tell the students that by examining some verses from Torah, we may better understand the connection between the holiday of Shavuot and the life-cycle stage of confirmation.
2. Instruct the students to look at Exodus 24:3, 4, and 7 as well as the portion from Torah that describes the festival of Shavuot (Numbers 28:26-31; Deuteronomy 16:10-12).

3. Ask the students to read and analyze both selections.

4. Explain that one of the texts they are looking at describes an early "confirmation," while the other describes the festival of Shavuot, on which confirmation is generally celebrated.

5. Have students work in pairs to think of parallels between Shavuot and confirmation.

6. List the following words and phrases to help the students:

> Celebration of acceptance
>
> Community
>
> Commitment
>
> Public reaffirmation

7. Based upon their study, ask each pair to answer the question: Why is confirmation traditionally celebrated in conjunction with the festival of Shavuot?

CHAPTER REVIEW

Materials: Chapter review worksheet from appendix sheet 9; pencils.

1. Photocopy the chapter from appendix sheet 9 (p. 86), and distribute it to the students.

2. Allow the students to work in pairs to complete the review.

3. When all the pairs are done, call on the students to help answer the questions aloud. Answers:

   1. Berlin; thirteen
   2. Reform or graduation; bar/bat mitzvah.
   3. Fifteen
   4. *Gemilut chasadim*
   5. Shavuot; Torah
   6. *Mitzvah*

CLOSURE

1. Explain to the students that although the custom and ceremony of confirmation is very new, it is an important part of the Jewish life cycle in the Reform Jewish community.

2. Ask the students to suggest terms and concepts related to confirmation to add to "The Jewish Life-Cycle" diagram.

3. Tell the students that this ongoing commitment need not cease when formal Jewish learning opportunities are no longer available at one's synagogue.

4. Explain to the students that the next chapter will explore all the ways Jewish people can be involved in the Jewish community without sitting in a classroom.

5. Ask the students to suggest examples of adults they know who are involved in Jewish learning and/or the Jewish community. What do these people do? When? Where? Ask the students to try to imagine why these adults choose to do so.

FAMILY ENRICHMENT

PERSONAL JOURNAL ACTIVITY

1. Send the students home with copies of the journal activity worksheet from appendix sheet 10 (p. 87) for themselves and their parents.

2. Explain that this assignment is designed to help them think about some of the connections they will explore between bar/bat mitzvah and confirmation.

3. Have the students write their answers in their journals, and suggest that they may wish to look at this entry from time to time to see how their ideas are changing and developing.

4. Encourage the parents to discuss their answers with their children.

5. Teachers and educators may want to revise this worksheet to ensure that their synagogue's particular issues and ideals will be reflected on the worksheet.

6. Instruct the students to add the material to their family album.

RESOURCES

Encyclopaedia Judaica. Jerusalem: Keter
Publishing House, Jerusalem Ltd., 1972.

Making Jewish Choices

CHAPTER SUMMARY

This chapter differs from the previous ones in that it does not explore a particular moment in the Jewish life cycle. Rather, the chapter explores the range of choices that are available to young adults as they leave the home of their parents and begin to create Jewish homes of their own. The chapter deals with Jewish spirituality, finding a Jewish community, building a personal connection to Israel, creating a Jewish home, dietary practices, hospitality, charitable acts, world repair, visiting the sick, and other issues related to the care of God's creation.

INSTRUCTIONAL OBJECTIVES

1. Investigate a variety of ways in which the students can be involved as active members of the Jewish community as they grow toward adulthood.
2. Examine the *mitzvot* of *gemilut chasadim*, *tikkun haolam*, and *tzedakah*.
3. Enable the students to explore their own goals for future Jewish observance and involvement.
4. Discover ways in which the Jewish community, its organizations, and its establishments can guide the students in establishing an active and meaningful Jewish life.

KEY TERMS

Bal Tashchit	Literally "do not destroy," a commandment to preserve God's creations by guarding against anything that may wantonly destroy nature.
Bikkur cholim	The mitzvah of visiting the sick.
Chanukiah	The nine-branch candelabra that is lit during Chanukah.
Chavurah	A group of Jewish friends who meet to pray, study, and celebrate together.
Gemilut Chasadim	Deeds of loving-kindness.
Gut Shabbes	Shabbat Shalom in Yiddish.
Hachnasat Orechim	The mitzvah of hospitality.
Haggadah	The special book for Passover that contains all the readings and songs of the seder.
Hamotzi	Traditional blessing over bread.
Havdalah	The ceremony of separation that marks the end of Shabbat and the beginning of a new week.
Hillel	the international Jewish organization for college and university students that sponsors on-campus opportunities for learning and worship.

Kashrut	The practice of maintaining Jewish dietary laws.
Kavanah	The Hebrew word for "intention," the practice of observing *mitzvot* with great focus.
KESHER	The UAHC college outreach program that connects college youth to the Reform movement.
Kiddush	Shabbat blessing that sanctifies wine.
Lulav and *etrog*	Bundled tree branches and a citrus fruit that are ritual objects used in the observance of Sukkot.
Mezuzah	A decorative case that contains a small scroll of parchment with the words of the *Shema* and *Ve'ahavta* prayers. A *mezuzah* is traditionally affixed to the doorpost of Jewish homes.
Shehecheyanu	Literally, "the One who has kept us alive;" the blessing said at all beginnings and very special moments in a person's life.
Teshuvah	Repentance.
Tikkun Haolam	Repair of the world.
Tzedakah	Literally, "righteousness;" the commandment to help those in need.

OPENING
(10 minutes)

Materials: Map of your city; pad of paper; tourist garb.

1. Dress up to resemble a stereotypical tourist.
2. Carrying a map of your city or the town closest to the religious school, enter the classroom a few moments after the usual start time (you may want to have a parent or another teacher greet students as they enter and monitor the classroom until you arrive).
3. Wander in and appear confused as you look around and continue to consult the map.
4. Look up and notice the students.
5. Explain that you have just started college/university in the area and you would like to find out how to get in touch with all the Jewish resources that are in town.
6. Take out a pad and paper, and ask the students to list as many of the Jewish sites, shops, and communal agencies or organizations as they know of in the area.
7. List their answers on the board.
8. When you feel that they have mentioned all they can, stop pretending to be new in town and explain that when a young Jewish person moves to a new city or town, he or she might want and need to find out where the Jewish resources are.
9. Explain that choosing to be connected to the Jewish community is one way of establishing a Jewish life.
10. Tell the students that this chapter of the textbook is not about a specific life-cycle ceremony; however, it is about a major stage in one's life, a time of making choices and consulting maps.

CLASSROOM ACTIVITIES

UNDERSTANDING OUR STORY
(30 minutes)

Materials: Map of Eurasia.

1. Bring to class a map of Europe and Asia.
2. Ask the students to locate the city of Alma-Ata.

3. Have the students read the story on pages 70-72.
4. Lead the students in a discussion by asking the following questions:
   - After her family moved to Alma-Ata, Natasha went without Shabbat for a long time. What finally motivated her to try to celebrate Shabbat once again?
   - Compare the celebrations of Shabbat in Natasha's old home and in her new home. How were they different? How were they the same? Describe, in particular, how the old and the new celebrations might have felt. Which do you think was better? Explain.
   - Describe a unique Shabbat experience you have had.
   - Try to imagine your life ten years from now. What would be your ideal living situation? How do you think you might be celebrating Shabbat in ten years?
   - If someone took away your Jewish life, what would you miss most? What might you do to get this part of your Judaism back (or think of creative alternatives)?

FOCUS: LIVING A JEWISH LIFE AND JEWISH SPIRITUALITY
(10 minutes)

Materials: Writing paper and pencils.
1. Ask the students to define the term "freedom of religion."
2. Ask students whether they think they have freedom of religion.
3. Explain to the students that living in a country that allows everyone the freedom to believe and practice any religion they want means that people have to make good choices. Even though we are Jewish by virtue of the fact that we are born Jewish, we need to make a special and conscious effort to live a Jewish life. Ask the students to explain why that is so.

4. Have the students read the Focus sections "Living a Jewish Life" and "Jewish Spirituality" on pages 72-73 of the textbook.
5. Invite the students to suggest definitions for the term "spirituality" as it used in this section of the book. What makes spirituality Jewish?
6. Distribute a blank sheet of paper to each student.
7. Instruct the students to write one way in which they live a Jewish life that is also spiritual. Next ask the students to write one Jewish behavior they are not currently doing but that they believe would provide them with greater spirituality.
8. Discuss with the students the possibility of their trying to observe their desired new behavior.

THE JEWISH HOME
(30 minutes)

Materials: Textbook, paper, pencils

1. Have the students read the section "The Jewish Home" on page 73 of the textbook.
2. Explain to the students that Jewish tradition teaches that a *mezuzah* should be affixed to the doorpost at the entrance to each room in a new home within thirty days of moving in. There is a ceremony for the dedication of a house that includes affixing the *mezuzah*. This ceremony, called a *Chanukat HaBayit*, literally "a consecration of the house," uses the following symbols and *berachot*:
   Challah that is dipped in salt, blessed, and distributed to all those gathered.
   Berachah—Hamotzi

בָּרוּךְ אַתָּה יי
אֱלֹהֵינוּ מֶלֶךְ הָעוֹלָם,
הַמּוֹצִיא לֶחֶם מִן הָאָרֶץ.

Wine or grape juice, for the blessing, shared with each guest.

53

Berachah— Short *Kiddush*

בָּרוּךְ אַתָּה יי
אֱלֹהֵינוּ מֶלֶךְ הָעוֹלָם,
בּוֹרֵא פְּרִי הַגָּפֶן.

Torah commentary or a selection from the Bible.

Berachah—Prayer relating to Jewish study

בָּרוּךְ אַתָּה יי
אֱלֹהֵינוּ מֶלֶךְ הָעוֹלָם,
אֲשֶׁר קִדְּשָׁנוּ בְּמִצְוֹתָיו
וְצִוָּנוּ לַעֲסוֹק בְּדִבְרֵי תוֹרָה.

Mezuzah with kosher parchment scroll.

Berachah—Prayer for affixing a *mezuzah*.

בָּרוּךְ אַתָּה יי
אֱלֹהֵינוּ מֶלֶךְ הָעוֹלָם,
אֲשֶׁר קִדְּשָׁנוּ בְּמִצְוֹתָיו
וְצִוָּנוּ לִקְבּוֹעַ מְזוּזָה.

Shehecheyanu

בָּרוּךְ אַתָּה, יְיָ אֱלֹהֵינוּ, מֶלֶךְ הָעוֹלָם,
שֶׁהֶחֱיָנוּ וְקִיְּמָנוּ וְהִגִּיעָנוּ לַזְּמַן הַזֶּה.

These items symbolize the following:

Challah	That there will always be food in the house.
Salt	An ancient symbol of wealth. When we dip *challah* in salt, we are suggesting that not only food, but abundant food and wealth will be found in the new home.
Wine or Grape Juice	The fruit of the vine is a symbol of joy and happiness.

Torah commentary or Hebrew Bible	Symbols of Jewish learning and commitment to one's Jewish heritage.
Mezuzah	Symbol of Jewish belonging.

Additional items that may be used:

Honey	For sweetness (*Challah* is dipped in honey).
Candlesticks	The wish that an atmosphere of Shabbat will always be in the home.
Havdalah spice box	The wish that all the different people who enter the home will be at peace with one another, just as the different spices mix to create a wonderful aroma.
Candles that are lit	The wish that the light will help all who enter the home see God more clearly.

The new homeowners may choose to find or write special prayers to embellish the ceremony.

3. List all of these elements on the board (or provide a list with the terms on paper).
4. Review each item on the list.
5. Group the students into pairs.
6. Instruct the pairs to create a ceremony for the consecration of a new home based on the symbols and *berachot* listed above.

BUILDING A JEWISH LIBRARY

Materials: Library questionnaire from appendix sheet 11.

1. Have the students read the section "Building a Jewish Library" on pages 73-74 of the textbook.
2. Prearrange a visit to the religious school or synagogue library. If there is a library resource teacher, ask that this person be available to the students during the visit to answer questions and make a presentation to the class about the development of a Jewish library.

3. Using the library questionnaire from appendix sheet 11 (p. 88) have the students do an "inventory" of the books that are in the library.

4. When the students have finished, return to the classroom and share answers.

KASHRUT—DIETARY CODES
(50 minutes)

Materials: Samples of food products.

1. Prior to this session, provide students with several examples of the most popular kosher seals.

2. Ask the students to explore their own home pantries for one example of a product with each of these symbols.

3. Ask students to bring samples to class.

4. Review the products they found.

5. Have the students read the section "Kashrut—Dietary Codes" on pages 74-75 of the textbook.

6. To conduct a further investigation of *kashrut*, invite a synagogue officer or the rabbi to class to explain the synagogue's *kashrut* policy and the decision-making process that led to this policy. Alternatively, invite to the class someone who keeps kosher, and have the students conduct an interview.

7. At the conclusion of this presentation (either one), arrange a debate on keeping kosher at home or keeping kosher in the synagogue.

8. Divide the class into two groups, one "for," the other "against."

9. The students should take ten minutes to prepare their arguments, based upon the presentation as well as the biblical texts mentioned in the book.

10. Each group should be given two minutes to present their arguments and one minute of rebuttal. The teacher should serve as judge.

11. Conclude this activity by asking the students what they think they would do in their own home. Ask them to explain their choice.

12. Collect all the sample products the students brought in and give them to a local food pantry or homeless shelter.

HACHNASAT ORECHIM—HOSPITALITY
(30 minutes)

Materials: Bible, paper, crayons, markers, pencils.

1. Have the students read the section "*Hachnasat Orechim*—Hospitality" on pages 75-76 of the textbook.

2. Group the students into pairs.

3. Distribute a Bible to each pair.

4. Instruct them to open their Bibles to Genesis 18:1-8 and read the narrative in which Abraham welcomes three strangers into his home. Explain that this is the basis for the *mitzvah* of *hachnasat orechim*, hospitality.

5. Ask the students to answer the following questions:
   - According to the text, who came to visit Abraham and Sarah?
   - How does Abraham respond to the visitors; what actions does he take?
   - How does Sarah respond to the visitors; what actions does she take?
   - What do you think the visitors were thinking when they saw Abraham and Sarah's actions?

6. Ask the students to draw a cartoon of the scene with a caption containing the thoughts of one of the following people: Sarah, Abraham, one of the strangers, God.

7. Have the students share their cartoons, and continue with the following questions:
   - Describe a time when you have were new. Describe how it felt.
   - What helped you to stop feeling new? Think of a person or event that was most helpful to you or other members of your family. Describe what was done (or what happened).
   - When have you welcomed a stranger?

Describe what you did.

- How are strangers welcomed into your synagogue and/or religious school? (There may be someone from the temple's new member committee or the school board who could visit and make a presentation on this last question.)

GEMILUT CHASADIM
(20 minutes)

Materials: Handouts from appendix sheets 12 and 13.

1. Have the students read the section "*Gemilut Chasadim*—Deeds of Loving-kindness" on pages 76-77 of the textbook.
2. Tell the students that one way to determine how you can best observe the *mitzvah* of *gemilut chasadim* is to reflect on the way that others could help you to improve your life. Distribute the *gemilut chasadim* worksheet from appendix sheet 12 (p. 89).
3. Ask the students to fill out the first part of the sheet individually.
4. When they are done, instruct the students to look at their answers.
5. Ask the students to think about the special things they know about their family members and friends and to make a list of things they could do for them to perform the *mitzvah* of *gemilut chasadim*.
6. Instruct them to fill out the second part of the *gemilut chasadim* worksheet.

TIKKUN HAOLAM—
REPAIRING THE WORLD
(20 minutes)

Materials: Map of the world (appendix sheet 13) cut into puzzle pieces totaling the number of students.

1. Copy the map of the world found in appendix sheet 13. (p. 90)
2. Cut the map into pieces so that there is one

piece for each student in your class. The pieces should resemble puzzle pieces.
3. Distribute one piece to each student in the class.
4. Ask the students to read the section "*Tikkun Haolam*—Repairing the World" on page 77 in the textbook.
5. Give the students a few moments to think of one way in which they could observe the *mitzvah* of *tikkun haolam*.
6. Instruct the students to write their idea on the back of their "puzzle" piece.
7. Invite each student to read his or her idea aloud to the class and then to come to the front of the class and tape his or her piece to the board.
8. As each student comes forward, it will be necessary to find where the puzzle piece fits. At the end of this activity, the world should appear whole.
9. Explain to the students that we all hold in our hands the potential to repair the world. We all just have to get out there and do it!
10. Where applicable, tell the students that they will have an opportunity to commit themselves to *tikkun haolam* with their families (see Family Enrichment p. 59).

TZEDAKAH—
HELPING THOSE IN NEED
(20 minutes)

1. Have the students read through the section "*Tzedakah*—Helping Those in Need" on page 77 of the textbook.
2. If the class is not already engaged in *tzedakah* collection and distribution, explore the ways in which you can begin doing so. Consider creating a class *tzedakah* box (perhaps based upon the puzzle pieces created in the previous activity).
3. In addition, if you have not yet used it, consider assigning "Family Enrichment, *Tzedakah* and the Family" from chapter 5.

BIKKUR CHOLIM—VISITING THE SICK
(15 minutes)

1. Ask the students if they have ever visited someone who is sick.

2. For those who have, ask what they did when they got there, how they felt about the visit, how they think the "patient" felt about the visit, and what they thought when the visit was over. What, if anything, did they learn about *bikkur cholim* from the experience? Were they scared, nervous, comfortable, uncomfortable, excited? Why?

3. Tell the students that Jewish tradition teaches us that *bikkur cholim*, visiting the sick, is one of Judaism's highest values. Why do they think that is so?

4. Have the students read the section "*Bikkur Cholim—Visiting the Sick*" on page 78 of the textbook.

BAL TASHCHIT—DO NOT DESTROY
(30 minutes)

Materials: Chart on appendix sheet 14.

1. Tell the class that Judaism values all of God's creation. In our traditional laws and customs, we have strict commands about preserving nature and caring for the environment.

2. Have the students read the section "*Bal Tashchit— Do Not Destroy*" on page 79 of the textbook.

3. Explain that one of the ways in which we preserve the environment is by using less of our resources. We can reduce, reuse, and recycle.

4. Distribute a copy of appendix sheet 14 (p. 91) to each student.

5. Explain to the students that the purpose of this activity is to understand how we can become active recycling agents. To do this, we begin by making a "recycling audit." Instruct students to check off all the items that they use on a regular basis at home, at

school, and at work. (Tell the students to ask their parents to help by explaining what they do when they are at work.) Tell the students that in many cases it is possible to substitute reusable things for disposables.

6. Looking at their audits, the students are to make a plan for switching to as many reusable products as possible. Encourage the students to talk to their parents about changing their habits.

7. You may want to have the class compose a letter that explains Jewish value of *Bal Tashchit* and asks families to begin a new program of reducing, reusing, and recycling.

8. The class may also want to establish a religious school recycling program.

FINDING A JEWISH COMMUNITY
(30 minutes)

Materials: Worksheet from appendix sheet 15.

1. Photocopy the worksheet from appendix sheet 15 (p. 92) and distribute one to each student.

2. Instruct the students to complete the worksheet by matching the "Jewish Needs" in List A with the "Jewish Organizations" in List B. The correct answers are as follows:

List A: Jewish Needs:
- Need for kosher meat
- Cemetery
- *Minyan* for saying *Kaddish*
- Ordained rabbis and trained cantors
- Money to start businesses/help new immigrants
- Place to buy Jewish books/ritual items
- Some way to help other Jews settle in the area
- Protection from anti-Semitism
- Make friends with other religious groups
- A place to meet other Jews
- Health care facility with kosher food
- A way to help poor Jews
- A way to communicate in the language spoken by the local Jewish community

- Jewish education of children
- Place for Jewish young people to meet

List B: Jewish Organizations:
- Kosher Butcher's Society
- Jewish Burial Society
- Synagogue
- Seminary to train rabbis and cantors
- Jewish loan society/bank
- Judaica store
- Jewish Immigration Society
- Political group to support Jewish rights
- Interfaith organization
- Jewish community center
- Jewish hospital/nursing home
- Jewish Aid organization
- Jewish newspapers in a variety of languages
- Jewish day school/after school programs
- Jewish camps/youth groups

3. As a class, create a column C, with the names of the local institutions and organizations that provide the services indicated.

4. As a resource, use local Jewish newspapers, temple bulletins, Federation bulletins, and local yellow pages.

GETTING POLITICALLY ACTIVE
(20 minutes)

1. One of the Jewish choices we can make involves getting politically active to support Jewish rights and to fulfill the Jewish value of helping others.

2. Find out about the issues in your area (perhaps the synagogue is involved in a campaign). Contact the Religious Action Center in Washington, D.C. at (202) 387-2800 or go on-line at "www.cdinet.com/rac" to determine some national issues about which the Reform Jewish movement has taken a stand.

3. Discuss a range of possible issues, and vote as a class to adopt one issue.

4. Together, write a letter in support of a worthy cause.

TEXTS ABOUT LIVING A JEWISH LIFE
(30 minutes)

Materials: Art supplies; copies of appendix sheet 16.

1. Ask students to read the following short Jewish texts, each of which represents an important Jewish value or idea.

2. Invite each student to choose one text for which they will draw an illustration.

3. Hand out the sheet of texts from appendix sheet 16 (p. 93).

4. As students create their symbols and drawings, have them label them with the concept that is being depicted. [E.g.: maintaining a Jewish library, engaging in Jewish study, commitment to ecological conservation, involvement in social action, connection to the Jewish community, supporting Israel, being hospitable, maintaining a Jewish home, attending synagogue, engaging in deeds of loving-kindness, etc.]

5. When the students are done, invite them to share their drawings and explain why they chose the particular text.

CHAPTER REVIEW

1. Write the words "Choices" and "Resources" side by side on the board.

2. Draw a line between them.

3. Ask the students to recall some of the adult Jewish choices presented in the chapter, and list them under "Choices" as they are mentioned.

4. Then ask the students to think of some of the resources that would be helpful to a young adult as he or she makes these Jewish choices. Though certainly not exhaustive, the following is an example of a list:

Choices	Resources
Jewish study	Jewish/synagogue library, Hillel, Jewish bookstore, synagogue adult education courses, Jewish bookclub, the Internet
Bal Tashchit	Jewish environmental organizations
Giving to or going to Israel	ARZA or WZO
Observe Shabbat	Judaica shop for ritual items, Jewish bakery, Jewish cookbooks; synagogue for worship and community celebrations
Affix a *Mezuzah*	Judaica shop, Jewish library to find appropriate prayers
Observe *kashrut*	Jewish bakery, kosher butcher, kosher cook books
Gemilut chasadim	Jewish organizations that identify needy causes

CLOSURE

1. Ask the students to recall the ways in which young adults can express and enhance their Jewish identity and live a life committed to Jewish activities and the Jewish community.

2. Using the words and concepts that they suggest, fill in a new section of "The Jewish Life-Cycle" diagram.

3. Tell the students that there are many other ways than were mentioned in the book that they will hopefully encounter and explore as they grow into adulthood.

FAMILY ENRICHMENT

TIKKUN HAOLAM MISHPACHTI—

FAMILIES REPAIRING THE WORLD

1. Send home background material on *tikkun Haolam* and appendix sheet 17 (p. 94).

2. Ask families to complete the activity and send the sheet back to class.

RESOURCES

Adahan, Miriam. *Raising Children to Care: A Jewish Guide to Child Rearing*. New York: Philip Feldheim, Inc., 1988.

Goldin, Barbara Diamond. *Creating Angels: Stories of Tzedakah*. Northvale, N.J.: Jason Aronson, 1996.

Lewis, Barbara. *The Kid's Guide to Social Action*.

Siegel, Danny. *Tell Me a Mitzvah: Little and Big Ways to Repair the World*. Kar-Ben, 1993.

Religious Action Center, Washington, D.C. (202) 387-2800 [on-line at: www.cdinet.com/rac].

Jewish Marriage

CHAPTER SUMMARY

This chapter presents Jewish marriage customs
and laws. The holiness of marriage is stressed in
terms of the relationship of the bride and groom
and the role of God in the wedding ceremony
and the marriage. The chapter ends by explaining
the Jewish traditions for divorce.

INSTRUCTIONAL OBJECTIVES

1. Discover how Jewish people from ancient
   times until present day have found marriage
   partners.
2. Examine some biblical marriages.
3. Explore God's role in sanctifying the
   ceremonies of Jewish marriage and divorce.
4. Learn both ancient and contemporary Jewish
   wedding customs and ceremonies.

KEY TERMS

Badeken di kalah A prenuptial ceremony in
which the groom raises and
lowers the bride's veil, based
upon the story in which Jacob
marries Leah instead of Rachel.

Betrothal — Now incorporated into the
wedding ceremony, it was
originally the ceremony of
engagement of the groom and
bride.

Chatan	Groom.
Chupah	A portable tent with four poles that serves as the wedding canopy under which the bride and groom are joined in marriage.
Eid/eidem	Witness/witnesses.
Get	The "certificate" of divorce.
Kalah	Bride
Ketubah	The marriage contract.
Kiddushin	Stemming from the root K/D/SH meaning "holy"; the Hebrew term for marriage.
Shadchan	Matchmaker.
Sheva Berachot	The seven blessings that are traditionally recited at the wedding and for seven days afterward.
Yichud	Literally, "seclusion"; a few quiet moments that the bride and groom spend alone as a couple after the marriage ceremony before they celebrate with their guests.

OPENING

Materials: Personal advertisements from a Jewish
news source; index cards.

1. Cut out the "personal" section of a Jewish
   newspaper. (If one is not available, go on-line
   to http://personalspage.com/personals/expo-
   nent, and print the personal advertisements.)

2. Select interesting and varied advertisements, enough for one for each student in the class.

3. Enlarge the advertisements on a photocopy machine, and paste each separate one on an index card.

4. As students enter the classroom, hand each one an index card on with a personal ad.

5. Instruct the students to read their cards aloud. Ask the students what they think they are reading.

6. Ask the students what it is that makes them like their friends. Is it that they like to do the same activities? Share the same hobbies? Come from similar families? Are their friends different from themselves in ways that they find interesting?

7. Explain to the students that it is difficult for many people, when they get older, to find other people with common interests whom they can date and potentially even marry. The personal ads are a way in which people look for potential marriage partners.

8. Ask the students if they know of other ways that individuals find others to date and build relationships. [blind dates, fellow workers or students, friends from childhood, etc.] Do any of them know how their parents met?

9. Tell the students that Jewish people have long been concerned with finding appropriate marriage partners for themselves, their family members, and their friends. This chapter will explore some interesting details about Jewish customs and traditions concerning marriage.

10. Conclude this opening exercise by asking the students to write their own personal ad looking for a friend. How would they describe themselves, and what would they be looking for in a friend?

11. Invite the students to share their ads.

CLASSROOM ACTIVITIES

UNDERSTANDING OUR STORY
(15 minutes)

1. Have the students read the story on pages 86-87 in the textbook. Ask the students what lessons we can learn from this legend. [There is a Divine role in finding a marriage partner.]

2. Ask the students if they agree or disagree that "marriage is made in heaven." Why? Have them explain their answers.

3. As a class, discuss God's role in marriage.

FOCUS: JEWISH DATING AND JEWISH MARRIAGE
(15 minutes)

Materials: Paper and pencils.

1. Ask the students if they know where and how their parents met. (If you are aware of a particularly difficult family situation or divorce, you may want to skip this part of the activity.)

2. Have some of the students share their parents' stories.

3. Instruct the students to read the section "Jewish Dating and Jewish Marriage" on page 88 of the textbook.

4. Ask the students to make two lists. One will be called "What Attracts People to Each Other," and the other will be called "Where People Can Meet Each Other."

5. Have the students break into pairs or small groups. Instruct the pairs or small groups to fill in the list with as many suggestions as they can think of, beginning with those ideas presented in the textbook.

TEXT STUDY
(40 minutes)

Materials: Simple items for costumes and props.

1. Have the students read the Text Study section on page 89 of the textbook. Ask them to consider the following questions:

- Do you think God had a role in the marriages of Isaac and Rebecca or Jacob and Rachel?
- Why do you think that Rebecca turned her face and covered herself?
- Why do you think Jacob did not know it was Leah instead of Rachel who came to him on his wedding night? What did Laban say was the reason he switched his daughters?
- What might Rebecca, Rachel, and Leah be thinking and feeling throughout this narrative?

2. Record some of the suggestions on the board.
3. Have the students break into two groups.
4. Assign one of the two biblical scenes to each group, and instruct the group to prepare a dramatic reenactment of their scene.
5. Encourage each group to embellish the scene by adding to the details that are presented in the biblical text. They may consider some of the suggestions that arose out of the earlier questions in this activity. Provide each group with some simple articles out of which they can make props and costumes.
6. Have the groups present their scenes to each other.

FOCUS: JEWISH MARRIAGE IS HOLY
(15 minutes)

1. Write the word *kiddushin* on the board both in Hebrew letters and in transliteration. Invite the students to read the word aloud.
2. Ask the students to think of other similar sounding words. [*Kiddush, Kaddish*] Ask the students if they know what it means. [sanctification, holy]
3. Ask the students to define "sanctification" and "holy." [special, set aside for special purpose, distinct]
4. Have the students read the Focus section "Jewish Marriage is Holy" on page 90 of the textbook.

5. Instruct the students to make a list of all the ways that marriage is *kadosh*, holy.

JEWISH WEDDING CUSTOMS
(10-30 minutes)

Materials: Chuppah, wedding photos, tracing paper, color and regular pencils.

1. Arrange for the class to view the temple's *chupah*. (In cases where the temple does not own one, teachers should attempt to bring in photos of weddings in which the *chupah* is visible.)
2. Prepare the class by reading the section "Jewish Wedding Customs" on pages 91-92 of the textbook.
3. After returning from seeing the synagogue's marriage canopy, distribute tracing paper and pencils (both lead and colored).
4. Ask the students to design a wedding canopy, incorporating both Jewish and personal symbols that are significant to them and represent the values they believe are embodied in the act of marriage.
5. You may supply the students with photographs or pictures of other wedding canopies for inspiration.
6. Invite the students to share their designs.

RAISING THE *CHUPAH*:
THEN AND NOW
(20 minutes)

1. Ask the students to view the pictures on pages 91 and 92 of the textbook. Each picture depicts a *chupah* raising.
2. Group the class into pairs.
3. Instruct each pair to compare and contrast the two pictures. What is the same in both pictures? What is different?
4. Ask the students to record any questions that they might have about the two pictures.
5. Share the comparisons when the students are finished, and allow the students to discuss any questions that they might have.

WHEN JEWISH MARRIAGES ARE PERFORMED
(15 minutes)

Materials: Several current Jewish calendars and one perpetual Jewish calendar.

1. Before the class session, ask parents to supply the student with the date of their marriage or that of another relative (e.g., grandparents).

2. Distribute calendars so that each student can see one.

3. Have the students read the blue-shaded section "Jewish Marriages Are Not Usually Performed on…" on page 92 of the textbook.

4. Ask the students to think of reasons why Jewish weddings are not held on those days. As you discuss the reasons, instruct the students to locate those days and periods on the calendar.

5. Some traditional reasons include:

   • Shabbat—it is not permitted to decrease the joy of either the wedding or the Shabbat by trying to celebrate both on one day; also, Jews may have to break some Shabbat observances to participate in or attend a wedding.

   • Rosh Hashanah, Sukot, Passover, Shavuot—similar reasons to Shabbat.

   • Yom Kippur—it would be inappropriate to celebrate a wedding on the most solemn day of the year, the day on which you are to be repenting; also, Jews may have to break some festival observances to participate in or attend a wedding.

   • The days between Passover and Shavuot—these are called the *sefirah*, the days when we "count" the *omer*, the forty-nine days between the second night of Pesach and Shavuot, with the exception of Lag Ba'omer, the thirty-third day; these days were considered a time of mourning for Rabbi Akiba's students.

6. Tell students that today, however, most Reform rabbis will perform a marriage on the days between Passover and Shavuot.

7. Using a perpetual Jewish calendar, ask the students to look up the secular date on which their parents (or other relative) were married.

8. Have the students note the Jewish date and year.

9. Using an "8 x 10" piece of paper, each student should make a square representing that date on the Jewish calendar.

10. The Jewish and secular dates should be written as well as symbols and pictures representing the season of Jewish and general life.

11. Post the squares to create a class marriage calendar.

BEFORE THE WEDDING
(15 minutes)

Materials: Sheets of blank paper.

1. Have the students read the section "Before the Wedding" on pages 92-93 of the textbook.

2. Instruct them to take a piece of paper and divide it into two lengthwise.

3. On the top of one side the students should write "*Ketubah* Signing," and on the top of the other side they should write "*Badeken Di Kalah*."

4. Ask the students to work independently and, using the textbook, record the details of either one of these events that take place before a wedding ceremony.

5. Have the students share their answers after they have had adequate time to write.

KETUBAH ARTISTS
(30 minutes)

Materials: *Ketubah* worksheet from appendix sheet 18; art supplies, large sheets of construction paper; *ketubah* reference books or catalogs.

1. Explain to the students that in this era many

North American Jewish couples use the *ketubah* as a way of capturing the special feelings they have as they begin their married life.

2. Some couples work with artists to design the artwork and wording of their *ketubah*. This is a way of creating a family heirloom, something that may be passed down in the family from one generation to the next and so on.

3. Tell the students that through this project they will gain some understanding of the important ideas and feelings that are part of a Jewish marriage. As they create the text and artwork for a *ketubah*, they will have a chance to think about relationships and ways in which Judaism is important to young couples.

4. Have the students complete this project in two parts. The worksheet found on appendix sheet 18 (p. 95) will help the students gather all the information they will need to create a *ketubah*.

5. Explain to the students that almost every *ketubah* contains certain standard information. Students can use information based on their parents' or a relative's wedding, or they can choose fictitious names, dates, and places. Certain phrases that appear in all *ketubot* are printed on the worksheet.

6. First have the students fill in the worksheet.

7. Then have the students follow the instructions for the parts that they are to write themselves.

8. Explain to the students that making a beautiful *ketubah* is an act of *hiddur mitzvah*, because it embellishes an object used in a sacred Jewish ritual and because it gives special pleasure to the bride and groom.

9. Invite the students to use a wide range of materials and mediums to create their *ketubot*, such as fabric, colored paper, special paints, markers and crayons, glitter, etc. Provide a reference book and/or some samples of *ketubot* to guide the students in creating their text for the *ketubah*.

LIFE-CYCLE BLESSINGS
(45 minutes)

Materials: Art supplies and blank white paper; pushpins or tape for displaying students' artwork.

1. Have the students read the *Sheva Berachot* on page 96 of the textbook. Divide the class into seven groups.

2. Assign each group one of the *Sheva Berachot*.

3. Instruct each group to illustrate their assigned *berachah*.

4. Provide the students with art supplies, and give them adequate time to set up, design and create their illustration, and clean up.

5. At the conclusion of this activity, have each group post their artwork so that the *Sheva Berachot* illustrations flow in succession from the first to the seventh.

6. Have each group present their ideas and recite their *berachah* to the class.

WHEN A MARRIAGE FAILS—DIVORCE
(15 minutes)

1. Introduce this section by stating that many families have experienced divorce. Assure the students that Judaism allows for marriages that do not work out as planned. Our tradition provides us with a ceremony to help us to dissolve marriages in a sacred way.

2. Have the students read the section "When a Marriage Fails—Divorce" on page 97 of the textbook.

3. Ask the students to identify one way that divorce may change how a family functions, both in the Jewish world and in the non-Jewish world. (Remember that some students will speak from experience and others from their imaginations.)

4. As you call on each student, note his or her response on the board. Where possible and appropriate, discuss the students' answers.

5. Using a Rabbis' manual, review with the students the elements of the ritual for Jewish divorce.

6. Review also the text of a *get* document (also found in the Rabbis' manual).

7. Discuss with the class how the document and the ceremony account for the feelings and changes that accompany a divorce.

8. Ask the class whether they think these rituals and documents would help people with the process of going through a divorce. Why or why not?

ARRANGED MARRIAGES

(15 minutes)

Materials: *Chumashim.*

1. Ask the students to define the term "arranged marriage." (They should remember from the story "Definitely in Heaven.")

2. Explain to the students that while marriages are generally no longer "arranged," this was the custom in biblical times.

3. Invite the students to discuss the pros and cons of arranged marriages.

4. Have the students read about Isaac and Rebecca's arranged marriage (Genesis 24:1-4). Ask the students to find evidence in the Torah that proves whether this arranged marriage was successful or unsuccessful.

CHAPTER REVIEW

(20 minutes)

Materials: List of vocabulary words.

1. The students have explored the ancient and modern customs involved in weddings. Have them look through a list of the vocabulary words that have come up in this chapter: *badeken di kalah, betrothal, chatan, chupah, eid/eidem, get, kalah, ketubah, kiddushin, shadchan, Shevah Berachot, yichud.*

2. Ask the students to write a letter as if they were describing a wedding that they have just attended. They should assume that the

recipient of their letter knows nothing about Jewish weddings.

3. Instruct the students to use at least seven of the twelve vocabulary words in their letter.

4. Invite the students to read their letters aloud.

CLOSURE

Materials: Blank pieces of paper; pens or pencils.

1. Distribute a small piece of paper to each student in the classroom.

2. Instruct the students to write down one detail about Jewish marriage that was new to them. Collect the pieces of paper, mix them up, and read the answers aloud.

3. Add these details, and other words and concepts that the students suggest, to the marriage section of "The Jewish Life Cycle" diagram.

4. Ask the students to look at the diagram. Point out that there is still one blank section.

5. Ask the students to think of what aspect of the life cycle has not yet been discussed. [death]

6. Explain that you will soon begin to study the rituals and customs surrounding dying, death, and mourning in the Jewish tradition.

JOURNAL ASSIGNMENT

Ask students to write a paragraph on what appeals to them about a Jewish wedding. Why does it appeal to them?

FAMILY ENRICHMENT

ASK THE CLERGY

1. Several weeks in advance, send home an invitation to parents to attend the class in which you will be teaching about the Jewish wedding.

2. In addition, have the rabbi or cantor come to visit the class to present the way he or she conducts a wedding ceremony.

3. Ask the students and their parents to compose three to five questions that they would like to ask the rabbi or cantor regarding how he or she prepares a couple for marriage, the wedding ceremony, or any other aspect of marriage about which they wish to inquire.

4. Allow the parents and students to ask their questions.

JEWISH MARRIAGE IN FILM

1. Ask families to rent a video in which Jewish marriage is depicted.

2. Families should view the film together and discuss the questions on appendix sheet 19 (p. 97).

RESOURCES

Isaacs, Ronald H. *The Bride and Groom Handbook*. West Orange, N.J.: Behrman House, Inc., 1989.

Lewittees, Mendell. *Jewish Marriage: Rabbinic Law, Legend, & Custom*. Northvale, N.J.: Jason Aronson Inc., 1994.

Marks, Susan. and Black, Bruce *Seven Blessings: Our Jewish Wedding Book*. New York: UAHC Press, 1997.

Sabar, Shalom. *Ketubah*. Philadelphia, PA: JPS, 1990.

Stopler, Pinchas. *Jewish Alternatives in Love, Dating and Marriage*. New York: National Conference of Synagogue Youth and University Press of America, Inc., 1984.

Death and Mourning

CHAPTER SUMMARY

This chapter deals with the final stage in the life cycle: death. Students will read about beliefs and customs related to death and mourning. The chapter focuses on the importance of memory and community in coping with death.

Teaching Note: Emphasis should be placed on death's being a part of the Jewish life-cycle. Assure the students that most people fear death and that it is natural to feel anxiety as the topic is discussed. It is critical to allow the students to express their own feelings. It is also advisable to ascertain if any student has recently experienced the death of a close relative or is living with a terminally ill family member.

INSTRUCTIONAL OBJECTIVES

1. Discover Jewish views and customs concerning death, burial, and mourning.

2. Explore the ways in which death is part of the cycle of life.

3. Reflect on deceased family members who have influenced the students and their families.

KEY TERMS

Chevrah Kaddisha	A specially trained volunteer that prepares the body for burial according to Jewish tradition.
Condolence call	A visit to the house of those mourning a relative in which the visitor attempts to bring comfort to the bereaved.
El Malei Rachamim	Literally, "God, full of compassion." A traditional prayer recited or chanted at the funeral in which the Hebrew name of the deceased is stated. The prayer invokes God's blessing and compassion on the soul of the deceased.
Ethical will	Written guidelines for living a moral life that one composes and then leaves for his or her offspring.
Hesped	"Eulogy," a short speech that honors the life of the deceased. It is usually delivered by the person leading the funeral service or by a close relative or friend of the deceased.
Kaddish Yatom	Mourner's Kaddish.
Keriah	The custom of tearing the garment or wearing a symbolic piece of torn cloth as an outward sign that one is in mourning for a relative.
Kevod hamet	Literally, "honor for the dead;" showing respect for the dead by respectfully handling and burying their bodies.
Seudat havra'ah	"Meal of consolation," the meal

eaten by mourners after they have buried a relative.

Shacharit	The daily morning service.
Sheloshim	The thirty-day mourning period.
Shivah	The seven-day mourning period.
Shivah minyan	An ordinary evening service in which (traditionally) ten adults are gathered in the home of the bereaved to support them as they recite the *Kaddish Yatom*.
Tiheyeh nishmato/ nishmatah" tzerurah, bitzror hachayim	"May his/her soul be forever bound in the bond of eternal life;" the final words on a Jewish headstone.
Yahrtzeit	The yearly anniversary of a relative's death.
Yiddish	A contraction of *Yidish-daytsch*, which means Judeo-German, the language of most Ashkenazi Jews from the early Middle Ages until recent times.
Yizkor	A special memorial service held on Yom Kippur, Shemini Atzeret, the last day of Pesach, and Shavuot.

OPENING

(5 minutes)

Note: This assignment may even be made prior to class. Students can be asked to bring a copy of the lyrics or a cassette of the song to play for their peers.

1. Write the phrase "Sing Many Songs That You May Be Remembered" on the board. Ask the students what they think this statement might mean.

2. Write down their responses on the board.

3. Ask each student to think of one song that they feel best expresses who they are and how they live.

4. Share the answers.

5. Tell the class that they will continue by reading a story that is entitled "Sing Many Songs That You May Be Remembered."

CLASSROOM ACTIVITIES

UNDERSTANDING OUR STORY

(5 minutes)

1. Have the students look at their initial definitions of the phrase "Sing Many Songs That You May Be Remembered."

2. Ask the students if the title fits the story. Can they can think of other fitting titles?

3. Discuss with the students how it was that Lynn finally came to feel some comfort after the death of her grandmother.

FOCUS

(30 minutes)

Materials: *Gates of Repentance*

1. Ask the students to recall someone they have loved who died.

2. Ask the students to recall three things about this person that they enjoyed or three experiences they had with this person that have stayed with them.

3. Invite the students to share their recollections.

4. Have the students read the Focus section on page 102 of the textbook, which talks about the importance of memory in Judaism.

5. Discuss the questions that are posed in the fourth paragraph.

6. Have the students look at the liturgy for the *Yizkor* service on pages 491-493 of *Gates of Repentance*.

7. Divide the students into groups of two or three.

8. Ask the students to determine three major themes that are embodied in the *Yizkor* liturgy.

9. Regroup the class, and record on the board all the themes that the students mention.

10. Distribute blank sheets of drawing paper and art supplies.

11. Ask each student to compose a collage of a deceased loved one that reflects their memories and the themes of the memorial liturgy.

12. Students should be encouraged to incorporate the words or themes of the liturgy into their collages.

JEWISH BELIEFS ABOUT LIFE AFTER DEATH
(20 minutes)

Materials: Art supplies.

1. Have the students read the section "Jewish Beliefs about Death and Life after Death" on page 102 of the textbook.

2. Explain to the students that no one really knows what happens after we die; but almost all religions have formed ideas and beliefs about what occurs. Remind the students that Judaism is an evolving religion where beliefs develop and change over the course of many years. Also, remind the students that an individual's belief about life after death may differ from the accepted belief of that person's religion.

3. Have the students read the section "Three Jewish Views of Life after Death" on page 103 of the textbook.

4. Ask the students what sounds most likely to them and what sounds least likely to them.

5. In addition, you may arrange a rabbinic

debate about the three views, with different groups of students arguing in support of each view.

FOCUS: JEWISH FUNERAL CUSTOMS
(15 minutes)

1. As a class, read the section "Jewish Funeral Customs" on pages 104-105 of the textbook.

2. Ask the students if they have ever seen particular Jewish funeral customs or remember hearing about them. (Note: Be sensitive to the fact that the students' memories may not serve them well and that some students may have attended the funerals of Christian relatives.)

3. Group the class into pairs, and ask each pair to consider the following questions:
   - What are the two principles that guide most Jewish funeral and mourning customs?
   - What does a *chevrah kaddisha* do?
   - When, according to Jewish custom, is a person to be buried?
   - On what days does Jewish custom prohibit burials? Why do you think that this is the case?
   - Where do funeral services usually take place?

4. To continue this exploration, you may arrange for the rabbi or a member of the synagogue's *shivah* committee to come and discuss funeral and mourning practices with the students.

5. Leave time for questions at the end.

UNDERSTANDING A JEWISH FUNERAL
(30 minutes)

Materials: Books and materials for research, or prepared biography.

1. Have the students read the section "Understanding a Jewish Funeral" on pages 105-106 of the textbook.

2. Ask the students what they think is the purpose and significance of a *hesped*.

3. Lead a discussion on what the content of a *hesped* might include.

4. Ask the students to consider whether there is anything that should not be mentioned in a *hesped*.

5. Choose several figures from Jewish history. This may require some library time for research, or you may choose to prepare brief biographies for the students to use as background. Select figures who are complex in their achievements (such as King David, Moses, Yitzhak Rabin, and Queen Esther). The point of this exercise is for students to consider how one memorializes and yet remains truthful to the deceased person's life.

6. List their names on the board.

7. Invite the students to select one person and write a *hesped* for that person.

8. Once the students are finished, read select pieces to the class.

LIFE-CYCLE BLESSINGS
(20 minutes)

1. Have the students review the life-cycle blessing: the *Kaddish Yatom*, the Mourner's *Kaddish*, on page 107 of the textbook.

2. Ask the students to suggest answers to the following:
   - What is the prayer asking for?
   - What characteristics does the prayer attribute to God?
   - What does the prayer hope for?
   - Who is included in the prayer?

3. Consult with the cantor or rabbi to find several different musical versions of the Mourner's *Kaddish* (e.g., the traditional chant, an arrangement by the group Safam).

4. Play the selections for the class.

5. Lead a discussion on how each version expresses the themes of the *Kaddish*.

6. Ask students to select a favorite version.

7. Invite the students to share their opinions.

FOCUS: SHIVAH
(20 minutes)

1. Ask the students if anyone knows what the term shivah or "sitting *shivah*" means. [The mourning period, usually of seven days, in which the bereaved remain at home and receive friends and relatives who come to console them.]

2. Instruct the students to take a piece of paper and write at the top: "Things that take place at the *shivah*."

3. Ask the students to read the section "*Shivah*" on pages 108-109 of the textbook and record all the things that mourners do while sitting *shivah*.

4. Lead a discussion with the class on the practice of sitting *shivah*.

5. Ask the students to suggest other things that might be appropriate to do when one is in the first week of mourning.

6. Review with the students the blue-shaded section "Things Not Done during the *Shivah* Period" on page 109 of the textbook. Ask the students if they would add or delete anything to or from the list.

7. Arrange for a member of the synagogue who has been trained to lead *shivah minyans* to speak with the students.

8. Ask the guest to especially discuss why he or she has chosen to perform this special *mitzvah* and how this responsibility feels.

AFTER THE SHIVAH PERIOD
(25 minutes)

Materials: Bibles, paper and pencils.

1. Have the students read the section "After the Shivah Period" on pages 109-110 of the textbook.

2. Ask the students to look at the photograph on page 110 of the textbook. Have they ever seen a Jewish cemetery or a Jewish section of a cemetery?

3. Based on the photographs and memories that they might have of cemeteries, what conclusions can they draw about Jewish headstones? [They are plain, they have Hebrew and English, they are mostly uniform in size, etc.]
4. Group the students into pairs.
5. Charge each pair with the task of creating tombstones for biblical characters.
6. Provide the students with Bibles.
7. Instruct the students to find information about various people in the Bible in order to create tombstones.
8. Each pair should create two tombstones with inscriptions. The final line should read *tav, nun, tzadee, bet, hay*, which stands for *Tiheyeh nishmato/nishmatah tzerurah, bitzror hachayim*—"May his/her soul be forever bound in the bond of eternal life."
9. Tell the students to use the following list to guide them in creating their tombstone inscriptions:
   * Hebrew name
   * Dates of birth and death (made up for the biblical characters)
   * His or her family role (father, brother, mother, etc.)
   * Some description of his or her greatest accomplishments
10. You may also arrange for a visit to a local Jewish cemetery (particularly an old one) for students to view the gravestones and do stone rubbings.

YAHRZEIT AND YIZKOR
(10 minutes)

Materials: Blank paper.

1. Bring a *Yahrzeit* candle to class, and place it at the front of the class where all the students can see it.
2. Ask if anyone has ever seen this object and knows how it is used.

3. Explain to the students that Judaism provides us with rituals that help us to remember relatives who have died. By marking the *yahrzeit* of loved ones, we keep their memory alive and have an annual reminder of their qualities and contributions.
4. Have the students read the section "*Yahrzeit* and *Yizkor*" on pages 110-111 of the textbook. Discuss why light is such an important symbol of Jewish memory.
5. Ask the students to divide a blank sheet of paper in half lengthwise from top to bottom.
6. On one side they should write "*Yizkor*," and on the other side they should write "*Yahrzeit*." Ask the students to compare and contrast the two rituals.
7. Ask the students to think about which is a more effective means of keeping a person's memory alive.

ETHICAL WILLS
(20 minutes)

Materials: Paper, appendix sheet 20, and a variety of writing instruments.

1. Have the students read the section "Ethical Wills" on page 111 of the textbook. Explain that an ethical will tells future generations what values were most important in a person's life. When one creates an ethical will and leaves it for future generations, one sends a part of oneself into the future. It's almost as though one is traveling through time to tell something very important to people who will live many years later. Once an ethical will has been created, it can be added to and modified at any time.
2. Explain to the students that they will work on a draft of an ethical will.
3. Provide the students with paper and a variety of writing instruments.

4. Ask the students to begin drafting their ethical wills by considering the questions from appendix sheet 20.

5. Encourage the students to use art and symbols to explain their ideas. Remind the students that the way in which they express their ideas can add extra meaning to their words. For example, if they wish to state that Jewish life-cycle rituals are an important way to mark life's stages, they could write the statement in a circle that has no beginning and no end; or they could write out all the life stages to symbolize the statement they are trying to make.

TEXT STUDY
(20 minutes)

Materials: Bibles or photocopies of textual pieces.

1. Group the students into pairs.

2. Each pair will examine a piece of sacred text that is customarily recited at or before a funeral (either by the rabbi or the mourners).

3. Distribute Bibles for the students to use, or hand out photocopies of the textual pieces. Choose texts from Malachai 2:6; Proverbs 21; Job 28:1-2, 12; Isaiah 40:6-8; 41:10; Psalms 15; 23; 24:1-6; 49; 73:26; 90; 91; 103:13-17; Jeremiah 8:18, 23.

4. Instruct the students to read the text assigned to them and consider the following questions:

   • What are the central themes in this text?

   • Are there any repeated words or phrases? What are they?

   • What might the author of this text have been feeling when he or she wrote it?

   • Do you think this text would be helpful to read at a funeral? Why or why not?

CHAPTER REVIEW

Materials: Photocopies of the exercise from appendix sheet 21.

1. Photocopy the exercise from appendix sheet 21 (p. 99), and distribute one to each student.

2. Instruct the students to match the correct term with its definition to review the important concepts discussed in this chapter. The correct answers are as follows:

Kevod Hamet	Respect for the dead
Pine	Type of wood used for Jewish coffin
Chevra Kaddisha	Jewish burial society
Shabbat	Funerals not permitted on this day
Keriah	Tearing of fabric by a mourner
Psalms	Special readings from the Bible
Eulogy	Speech that praises a person
Hesped	Hebrew word for "eulogy"
El Malei Rachamim	Prayer that asks for God's compassion
Kaddish	Prayer recited by the mourners

CLOSURE

1. Remind the students that while death is scary and often sad for the surviving relatives of the deceased, it is a necessary part of the life cycle.

2. Ask for suggestions of terms and concepts related to this stage of the life cycle to fill in the last remaining section of "The Jewish Life Cycle" diagram.

3. Emphasize that Judaism offers many rituals and customs that can help us to express our grief and cope with our loss.

4. Encourage the students to keep their textbooks in a place that is easily accessible so

that if they find themselves wondering about any of the customs or beliefs about death in Judaism, they can refer to their textbooks immediately. Also, recommend that the students discuss with their parents some of the particular rituals about which they have learned.

Note: As this is the final chapter of the textbook and the class has now finished studying the Jewish life cycle, consider having a *siyyum.* See notes in the introduction.

JOURNAL ASSIGNMENT

1. Have the students interview their parents about precious and meaningful heirlooms that have been passed from generation to generation.

2. Have the students bring in pictures or draw pictures depicting one or more item.

3. Have the students write descriptive paragraphs about the objects and any interesting story associated with them.

4. Instruct the students to think ahead to when they are older and their parents may entrust these precious items to them. How will they (the students) care for them, use them, and display them?

FAMILY ENRICHMENT

CEMETERY VISIT

1. Suggest to the parents that they visit a cemetery as a family. (Where possible, they should visit a Jewish cemetery or the Jewish section of a cemetery.)

2. Distribute the family enrichment activity worksheet from appendix sheet 22 (p. 100).

3. Have the parents support their child in some investigative work by setting up an interview with the director of the cemetery if possible.

The child could ascertain some of the following information (and anything else in which he or she is interested) and have the cemetery staff lead him or her to any unusual or remarkable headstones. The family could also try to answer the questions on their own.

- What is the name of the cemetery?
- When was it established?
- Which is the oldest grave marker?
- How many of the markers have Hebrew names, and how many English?
- What are the different choices for marker shapes and sizes?
- Who maintains the gardens and walkways?

4. The parents may wish to find out if the cemetery has special days on which the public can come to do gardening or cleaning and then arrange a return visit for their family to volunteer for this important mitzvah.

RESOURCES

Binder Kadden, Barbara, and Bruce Kadden. *Ethical Wills: Handing Down Our Jewish Heritage.* Denver, CO.: ARE.

Grollman, Earl. *Bereaved Children and Teens: A Support Guide for Parents and Professionals.* Boston: Beacon Press, 1996.

Riemer, Jack, ed. *Jewish Reflections on Death.* New York: Schocken Books, 1987.

Sonsino, Rifat and Daniel B. Syme. *What Happens After I Die?* New York: UAHC Press, 1990.

Techner, David and Judith Hirt-Manheimer. *A Candle for Grandpa: A Guide to the Jewish Funeral for Children and Parents.* New York: UAHC Press, 1993.

Wolfson, Ron. *A Time to Mourn, A Time to Comfort.* Woodstock, Vt.: Jewish Lights Publishing, 1996.

Appendix: Introduction

APPENDIX SHEET 1

SAMPLE LESSON PLANNER

This form may be reproduced and is designed to help the teacher develop an organized, coherent lesson plan for each chapter of *The Book of the Jewish Life*.

Lesson Plan for Chapter _____

_____

Teacher: _____   Class: _____

Date: _____

Focus

_____

_____

Instructional Objectives

Students will be able to:

_____

_____

_____

Materials

_____

_____

_____

_____

LESSON

Opening

_____ (time allotment:)

_____

_____

_____

Classroom Activities

_____ (time allotment:)

_____

_____

_____

_____

_____

_____

Chapter Review

_____ (time allotment:)

_____

_____

_____

Closure

_____ (time allotment:)

_____

_____

Family Enrichment

_____

Post Session Comments

_____

_____

Appendix
Chapter One

APPENDIX SHEET 2

JOURNAL ASSIGNMENT

Investigate your family traditions. By learning more about the past generations of your family and how your relatives celebrated the special stages of their lives, you will understand more clearly how and why certain family customs developed. You can even get ideas on how to help develop new and meaningful life-cycle rituals of your own!

Using this worksheet, interview your parents, grandparents, aunts, uncles, cousins, and close family friends. Although some relatives may no longer be alive, others will be able to help you with stories and facts.

MY FAMILY WORKSHHET

1. My parents were born in _____(city and country)
2. My grandparents were born in _____
3. My great-grandparents were born in _____
4. My family came to this country in _____(year) by _____(means of transportation) because _____
5. In my family, something Jewish that we have passed down from generation to generation is (what you write about does not have to be material) _____
6. Something Jewish that I would like to pass down to the next generation is _____
7. Three things that I would like my grandchildren to know about me are _____

Other questions

How have *you* ensured that future generations can learn about the present time and their family in this generation? _____

_____

_____

_____

_____

_____

_____

Appendix
Chapter Two

APPENDIX SHEET 3

HEBREW NAME WORKSHEET

Write your Hebrew name. Write it in English transliteration (English letters that follow the Hebrew sounds) and also in Hebrew letters.

My Hebrew name is _____

My parents' Hebrew names are _____ and

_____

My full Hebrew name is _____

My Hebrew name means _____

_____

Appendix: Chapter Three

APPENDIX SHEET 4

FAMILY ENRICHMENT ACTIVITY WORKSHEET

Please ask your parents to help you fill out this worksheet.

1. What berit ceremonies took place in your family? _____

_____

_____

_____

2. Interview your relatives about berit ceremonies that they remember. What was special about the ceremony? What was unique about the ceremony? In what way was it a traditional ceremony?

_____

_____

_____

_____

_____

3. Were you welcomed with a berit ceremony? What was it like? Who came? Where was it held? Are there any photographs to look at or a program of the ceremony?_____

_____

_____

_____

_____

4. Bring photographs or color photocopies of family berit ceremonies to school, and add them to your family album.

5. Create labels for the photos describing what is taking place and identifying the people in the photo.

6. Choose one anecdote of a family berit ceremony, and write about it in your family album.

Appendix: Chapter Five

APPENDIX SHEET 5

SOME PRIVILEGES AND RESPONSIBILITIES OF JEWISH ADULTS

_____ Being called up to the Torah for an aliyah

_____ Wearing a talit

_____ Being included in a minyan

_____ Fasting on Yom Kippur

_____ Lighting Shabbat candles yourself (boys as well as girls)

_____ Continuing your Jewish education

_____ Not gossiping or spreading rumors about others

_____ Giving tzedakah

_____ Feeding the homeless

_____ Attending synagogue services

_____ Teaching in a religious school

_____ Traveling to Israel

APPENDIX SHEET 6

BAR/BAT MITZVAH AS A TIME OF CHANGE

Discussion questions on Genesis 32:25-31:

1. Some people interpret this Torah passage as Jacob struggling with another human being and others say he struggled with an angel of God. After reading this Torah text, with whom do you think Jacob wrestled? _____

_____

_____

_____

_____

2. Do you think Jacob was the winner of the struggle? Why? Why not?

_____

_____

_____

_____

3. Some of the rabbis who have written commentaries on the Torah see Jacob's wrestling as a metaphor for his struggle to grow up and be an adult member of the Jewish community. Parents: As you look forward to your son/daughter becoming bar/bat mitzvah, what do you think will be your biggest challenge? Students: As you look forward to becoming bar/bat mitzvah, what do you think will be your biggest challenge?

_____

_____

_____

_____

APPENDIX SHEET 7

FAMILY TZEDAKAH ACTIVITY

Take turns reading the quotes. Discuss what you think each quote means. Do you agree or disagree with the quote? Why?

Discussion Questions

A. You shall not close your hand against your needy kinsman. Deuteronomy 15:7

B. *Tzedakah* outweighs all other religious precepts. Talmud, ***Bava Batra***

C. Even a poor man living on *tzedakah* should give *tzedakah*. Talmud, ***Gittin***

D. If you see a person giving liberally, it means his wealth will grow; if you see one who shuns *tzedakah*, it means her wealth will dwindle. ***Midrash Mishleh***

E. Who is kind to the poor lends to ***Adonai***. Proverbs 19:17

Setting Family Goals

Consider the following questions to continue your discussion:

1. What might be the connection between the celebration of life-cycle ceremonies and the giving of *tzedakah*? _____

    _____

2. What are ways that this family can make the giving of *tzedakah* a meaningful experience?

    _____

    _____

3. Design (and create) a family *tzedakah* box. Choose a prominent place to display this new family heirloom. Mark special moments throughout the year by making regular donations to the box. Once a year, sit as a family and decide how to distribute the money that has been collected.

Appendix: Chapter Six

APPENDIX SHEET 8

What Does Jewish Tradition Teach Us about Religious Education? _____

_____

_____

When they reach the age of five, children should _____

_____

_____

At age ten, they should _____

_____

_____

When children reach the age of thirteen, they are ready to _____

_____

_____

At fifteen, they should _____

_____

_____

APPENDIX SHEET 9

CHAPTER 6 REVIEW WORKSHEET

1. The first coed confirmation ceremony took place in _____. The boys and girls who were confirmed were _____ years old.

2. Confirmation was a _____ ceremony that temporarily replaced _____ for students graduating at the age of thirteen.

3. When bar and bat mitzvah were readopted by the Reform Movement, the age of confirmation was changed to _____ or older.

4. Holding a particular set of beliefs is not required for confirmation. However, as part of confirmation preparation, students are usually involved in a special confirmation curriculum. They often participate in a project of doing acts of loving-kindness called _____ in Hebrew.

5. Confirmation is tied to the festival of _____ because they both are connected to accepting the _____.

6. Lifelong study is an important _____ in Jewish life.

APPENDIX SHEET 10

JOURNAL ACTIVITY WORKSHEET

Explore the Connections between Bar/Bat Mitzvah and Confirmation

1. When I think about God, I _____

   _____

2. For me, being part of the Jewish community means _____

   _____

3. Some Jewish things that I do now are _____

   _____

4. I think that getting a Jewish education is _____because

   _____

5. My favorite episode in the Bible is _____because _____

   _____

6. The most important thing about **being Jewish** is _____

   _____

7. The most difficult thing about **being Jewish** is _____

   _____

8. The greatest problem facing Jews today is _____

   _____

9. Israel is important to me because _____

   _____

10. I think that Jews can help make the world a better place by _____

    _____

11. The best place to give *tzedakah* now is _____because

    _____

Note to students: Look at this entry from time to time to see how your ideas continue to change and develop.

Note to parents: Discuss your answers with your children.

Appendix: Chapter Seven

APPENDIX SHEET 11

LIBRARY QUESTIONNAIRE

What is the oldest book in the collection? _____

How many Bibles and biblical commentaries are in the collection? _____

_____

What are the reference books?_____

What are three recent most acquisitions? _____

_____

How many sections are there, and what are they? _____

How are the books classified? _____

Select one book from each section that you would like to own for your own Jewish library. Explain your

choices. _____

_____

_____

_____

_____

APPENDIX SHEET 12

GEMILUT CHASADIM WORKSHEET

Part 1. Ways in Which Others Can Help Me

1. I believe that my (mother, father, brother, sister—pick one) could help me by _____

_____

_____

2. My best friend could make me feel very good by _____

_____

_____

3. I would feel more self-confident in class if _____

_____

_____

4. When I feel sad, a person I care about could help me by _____

_____

_____

5. When I cannot handle everything, I need someone to _____

_____

_____

Part 2. Ways in Which I Can Help Others

1. To help my (mother, father, sister, brother—pick one) I could _____

_____

_____

2. I could be an extra good friend to my best friend by _____

_____

_____

3. I could help a student in my class feel more confident/more prepared in class by _____

_____

_____

4. I could help someone I know who is sad by _____

_____

_____

5. Someone I know needs special help. I can help that person by _____

_____

_____

APPENDIX SHEET 13

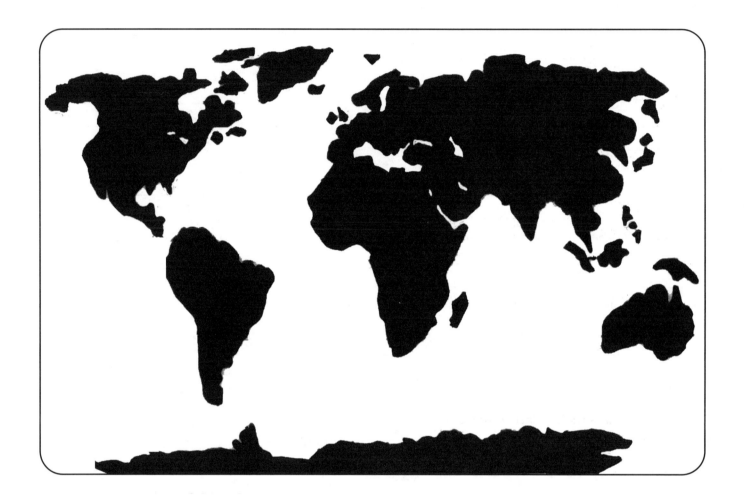

the world

APPENDIX SHEET 14

BAL TASHCHIT AND THE PRODUCTS WE USE

Product	At home	At school	At work
Paper cups			
Styrofoam cups			
Plastic cups			
Ceramic cups (nondisposable)			
Plastic wrap			
Foil wrap			
Plastic bags			
Reusable shopping bags			
Reusable cloth laundry bags			
Metal cans			
Glass bottles			
Plastic bottles			
Reusable beverage containers			
Recycled paper			
Nonrecycled paper			
Styrofoam take-out food cont.			
Reusable plastic food containers			
Reusable lunch carrier			
Metal eating utensils			
Plastic eating utensils			

APPENDIX SHEET 15

FINDING A JEWISH COMMUNITY

List A: Jewish Needs	List B: Jewish Organizations	List C
Need for kosher meat	Seminary to train rabbis and cantors	
Cemetery	Jewish community center	
Minyan for saying *Kaddish*	School programs	
Ordained rabbis and trained cantors	Jewish Burial Society	
Money to start business/ help new immigrants	Kosher Butcher's Society	
Place to buy Jewish books/ ritual items	Jewish loan society/bank	
Some way to help other Jews settle in the area	Interfaith organizations	
Protection from anti-Semitism	Jewish Aid organization	
Make friends with other religious groups	Jewish hospital/nursing home	
A place to meet other Jews	Judaica store	
Health care facility with kosher food	Synagogue	
A way to help poor Jews	Political group to support Jewish rights	
A way to communicate in the language spoken by the local Jewish community	Jewish day school/after school programs	
Jewish education of children	Jewish Immigration Society	
Jewish adult responsibilities	Jewish camps/youth groups	
Place for Jewish young people to meet	Jewish newspapers in a variety of languages	

APPENDIX SHEET 16

TEXTS ABOUT LIVING A JEWISH LIFE

"Keep your books well. Keep them from the rain above, from mice and any other damage, because they are your precious treasure." Yehuda ben Tibbon

"Let a man not say, "I will read that I may be called wise and study that I may be called a scholar, but do it out of love, and honor will come at the end." Talmud, *Nedarim*

"When you lay siege and battle against a city... you must not destroy its trees.... You may eat of them, but you must not cut them down." Deuteronomy 20:19

"Learn to do good; seek justice, work against oppression, defend the fatherless, plead for the widow." Isaiah 1:17

"All Jews are responsible each for the other." Talmud, *Shavuot*

"If I forget thee, O Jerusalem, let my right hand wither! Let my tongue cleave to my mouth if I remember thee not, if I prize not Jerusalem above all my joys." Psalm 137:5-6

"Hospitality matters more than greeting the Divine Presence." Talmud, *Shabbat*

"Is there any man who has built a new house but has yet to dedicate it? Let him go back to his home, lest he die in battle." Deuteronomy 20:5

"The synagogue is the sanctuary of Israel.... it has been to Israel, throughout our wanderings, a visible token of the presence of God in the people's midst." *Gates of Prayer*

"The world exists for the sake of kindness." Rashi

APPENDIX SHEET 17

TIKKUN HAOLAM MISHPACHTI—FAMILIES REPAIRING THE WORLD

Dear Parents:

Beginning a commitment to *tikkun haolam* is a very special occasion. It is traditional to ask for blessing when one begins an important new undertaking. The following is a prayer that was written specifically for such an occasion:

"Creator of the universe, You have implanted in us a spark of Your creative will. You have made us Your partners in the building of the world. In this task that I am about to begin I need clear vision and wise judgment. May I work with those I love in the light of Your presence and use all my powers for good works and for blessing. Amen."

From *On the Doorposts of Your House* CCAR, NY: 1994.

Survey the social action causes in your local area. You may want to go on-line to www.jtsa.edu/melton/tzedakah or www.clickonjudaism.org to get some ideas or help. Choose a *tikkun haolam* project in which your family can participate.

Write a brief description:

Our project is _____

_____

_____

Now, from what you learned about writing a prayer for a new project, write your own prayer for the success of your undertaking:

Introduction_____

_____

_____

How God helps us _____

What God wants us to do _____

Statement of one's special needs_____

Request for support by others _____

Request for support by God_____

Request for success _____

Closing_____

_____

_____

Appendix sheet: Chapter Eight

APPENDIX SHEET 18

KETUBAH WORKSHEET

1. Name of bride

   English: _____

   Complete Hebrew name (includes parents' Hebrew names):_____

   _____Example: Chayah bat Shamir ve Dina

   (Note: **Bat** means "daughter of"; Shamir and Dina are the parents of Chayah.)

2. Name of groom

   English: _____

   Complete Hebrew name (includes parents' Hebrew names):_____

   _____Example: Nisan ben Moshe ve Leah

   (Note: **Ben** means "son of"; Moshe and Leah are the parents of Nisan.)

3. Date of wedding

   Secular date: _____

   Jewish Date (day of the week, month, year): _____

   (Check a Jewish calendar for the Jewish date.)

4. Place of wedding (city, state, country): _____

Typical beginning for an egalitarian *ketubah*:

On the _____ day of the week, the _____ day of _____

Five Thousand Seven Hundred _____ years since the creation of the world as we

reckon here in _____ . The bride, _____ daughter of

_____ and _____ says to the groom:

With this ring you are consecrated unto me as my husband, according to the tradition of Moses

and the Jewish people.

The groom, _____ son of _____ and

_____ says to the bride: With this ring you are consecrated unto

me as my wife, according to the tradition of Moses and the Jewish people.

Typical ending for egalitarian *ketubah*:

Witness _____

Witness _____

Bride _____

Groom _____

Rabbi _____

APPENDIX SHEET 19

FAMILY ACTIVITY

Jewish Marriage in Film

Rent a video in which a Jewish marriage is depicted. View the film together, and discuss the following questions:

1. What did you learn from the film about Jewish weddings?

2. How does the film portray Jewish marriage in contrast to and in concert with what you learned in the textbook?

3. What did you like most about the film?

4. What did you like least about the film?

Suggested films:

Crossing Delancy

Fiddler on the Roof

Hester Street

Appendix: Chapter Nine

APPENDIX SHEET 20

ETHICAL WILLS

1. Some of the most important qualities in a person are _____

2. Being a good person means _____

3. Education is important because _____

4. Jewish education is important because _____

5. Some of the most important things in life are _____

6. Giving *tzedakah* is important because _____

7. A charity I really believe in supporting is _____ because _____

8. My favorite Jewish holiday is _____ because _____

9. If I could do anything to make the world a better place, I would _____

10. Honoring your father and your mother means _____

APPENDIX SHEET 21

DEATH AND MOURNING IN JUDAISM: A REVIEW OF TERMS

Match the correct term with its definition:

Kevod hamet	Jewish burial society
Pine	Funerals not permitted on this day
Chevra kaddisha	Tearing of fabric by a mourner
Shabbat	Type of wood used for Jewish coffin
Keriah	Respect for the dead
Psalms	Hebrew word for "eulogy"
Eulogy	Prayer recited by the mourners
Hesped	Special readings from the Bible
El Malei Rachamim	Speech that praises a person
Kaddish	Prayer that asks for God's compassion

APPENDIX SHEET 22.

FAMILY ENRICHMENT ACTIVITY WORKSHEET: VISITING A CEMETERY

Dear Parents,

As part of our study of death and mourning in Jewish tradition, we are asking that you help your child do some research. Please support your child in some investigative work by setting up an interview with the director of the cemetery if possible. In this way your child can ascertain some of the following information (and anything else in which he or she is interested) and have the cemetery staff lead him or her to any unusual or remarkable headstones. You can also try to answer the questions on your own.

What is the name of the cemetery?

When was it established?

Which is the oldest grave marker?

How many of the markers have Hebrew names, and how many English?

What are the different choices for marker shapes and sizes?

Who maintains the gardens and walkways?

You may wish to find out if the cemetery has special days on which the public can come to do gardening or cleaning and then arrange a return visit so that your family can volunteer for this important *mitzvah*.

Suggested Resources for Families

Binder Kadden, Barbara and Kadden Bruce. *Ethical Wills: Handing Down Our Jewish Heritage*.

Grollman, Earl. *Bereaved Children and Teens: A Support Guide for Parents and Professionals*.

Riemer, Jack, editor. *Jewish Reflections on Death*. New York: Schocken Books, 1987.

Sonsino, Rifat & Syme, Daniel B. *What Happens After I Die?* UAHC Press, New York, 1990.

Techner, David and Judith Hirt-Manheimer. *A Candle for Grandpa: A Guide to the Jewish Funeral for Children and Parents*. NY: UAHC Press.

Wolfson, Ron. *A Time to Mourn, A Time to Comfort*. Woodstock, NY: Jewish Lights, 1996.

NOTES

NOTES

NOTES

NOTES